In *Closing Times* the novelist and
publisher Dan Davin has set down
first-hand recollections of seven of his
friends, all writers, all recently dead:
Julian Maclaren-Ross, W. R. Rodgers,
Louis MacNeice, Enid Starkie, Joyce
Cary, Dylan Thomas, and the Yiddish
poet Itzik Manger. The worlds these
individuals inhabited were as diverse as
the settings of these memoirs: Fitzrovia
just after the war, Oxford, the BBC,
a P.E.N. congress in Edinburgh, the
Lower East Side in New York, a Dublin
pub. The unifying thread is Dan Davin's
own participation in the episodes
chronicled here, and his deep feeling for
his friends. 'I have been governed,' he
says in his Introduction, 'intuitively
more than consciously, by a principle of
inclusion that takes as primary the
personal relationship between my subject
and me, and by my own conception of
his character, what interested me about
him, what brought us together, what I
liked—or even loved—in him, what
I thought to be flaws . . .' The result is
in effect an informal autobiography, a
vivid and telling portrait of a literary
man in his time, as well as a moving
lament for 'the makers whom death has
unmade'.

⟩rn in New Zealand
ıts, and educated
ʹtago and Oxford.
War he served in
the British Army, and after 1940 as an
officer in the New Zealand Division, in
Greece, Crete, North Africa, and Italy.
He is the author of seven novels
published since 1945, the most recent
Not Here, Not Now (1970) and *Brides
of Price* (1972); he has also published a
collection of short stories—a second is
to appear shortly—and a volume of
military history, *Crete* (1953). A publisher
since 1945, Mr. Davin is a Fellow of
Balliol College, Oxford.

Dan Davin

CLOSING TIMES

London
OXFORD UNIVERSITY PRESS
New York   Toronto
1975

Oxford University Press, Ely House, London W. 1

GLASGOW NEW YORK TORONTO MELBOURNE WELLINGTON
CAPE TOWN IBADAN NAIROBI DAR ES SALAAM LUSAKA ADDIS ABABA
DELHI BOMBAY CALCUTTA MADRAS KARACHI LAHORE DACCA
KUALA LUMPUR SINGAPORE HONG KONG TOKYO

ISBN 0 19 212197 9

© Dan Davin 1975

Thanks are due to the editors of the magazines where some of these essays first appeared: *The London Magazine* for 'Good Night, Julian, Everywhere' and 'At the End of his Whether'; *Encounter* for 'In a Green Grave'; *The Cornhill* for 'The Chinese Box'. For permission to quote from *The Collected Poems of Louis MacNeice,* edited by E. R. Dodds (1966), I am indebted to the publishers, Faber and Faber Ltd., and to the Estate of Louis MacNeice.

D. M. D.

*Set in Great Britain by Gloucester Typesetting
Printed at The Pitman Press, Bath*

To

W.K.D.

*without whom there would have been
neither friends nor book*

CONTENTS

ILLUSTRATIONS

INTRODUCTION

One day about ten years ago I had half an hour to fill in before a lunch appointment. I had in my pocket the World's Classics edition of Johnson's *Lives of the Poets* and in the Turl Bar over a pint of bitter I began to read the life of Richard Savage which I hadn't looked at since before the war. I had read only a few pages when I realized that I knew a successor to Savage: Julian Maclaren-Ross, at that time still alive.

A few years went by and Julian, too, was dead. Not long after, I was again reading the *Lives*, this time in the big Birkbeck Hill edition and consecutively. I was again struck by the resemblance between Savage and Julian, but it also occurred to me how much better Johnson was when he was writing about poets he had actually known or was writing from a tradition of hearsay that was still detailed and fresh. Others of my writer friends, besides Julian, were at this time lately dead and the work they had left seemed good enough to ensure that another generation would be interested in the lives of those who wrote it.

It occurred to me also that I might, perhaps even should, set down my recollections of these friends and leave for some future Dr. Johnson the raw materials, a few living facts. At worst, or at best even, one would be providing contemporary evidence which might help to prevent a later generation of thesis-writers from going too wildly if solemnly astray, would be anticipating and forestalling some possible misunderstandings, the prim failures of charity with which the stainless academic is apt to afflict those dead before his time.

The task was congenial, since it meant recalling good times now gone; and pious, like the gesture of a soldier inverting a dead comrade's rifle in the sand above his grave, a temporary memorial. And I was of an age when one wants to do something to halt or at least delay the progress of oblivion, the darkening of the past which has already become the larger share of one's own lease of time. That sergeant had strictly arrested them; his warrant was already signed for me.

Moreover the circumstances in which I am usually constrained to write were favourable to the piecemeal nature of what I had in mind. These brief memorials could be written in those intervals of rapid concentration which were all I had time for, and did not require the steady continuous effort of months which one needs for a novel.

In the memoirs collected here I have aimed at displaying the man and not at criticizing the work. Criticism and aesthetic judgements date in a way that the work of art itself does not; or at least if a work of art is alive it will go on living however people's opinions of it change, whereas criticism usually dies with the fashion, the ambience, from which it arose. But the minor facts about a man, the trivial events and circumstances which were for him, if not the determinants, at least the conditions and components of what he wrote, vanish faster even than the views of critics; and yet they are often much more worthy of recall.

So, having had neither the time nor the wish to write complete biographies, I have restricted myself in the main to setting down what was already in my possession from personal knowledge, from memory, from private papers, from the occasional testimony of friends on whom I could rely for the essential truth of an anecdote or a conversation, even if not for its precise wording of report. I should admit by way of warning that my memory may here and there have been imposed upon by my imagination working in the murky retrospect and insinuating the sort of created truth which is *ben trovato* rather than in the strictest sense well founded.

Through many of the years in which these friendships were lived I kept a sort of sporadic diary. It is a disappointing aid; for it is often silent altogether and, still oftener, enigmatic: I evidently thought that a few essential clues would stimulate my memory to the reconstruction of whole scenes and conversations, when I ought to have known that broken-winded old grey mare better and what a small burden she could carry. Still, the diary is reliable for dates at least, and sometimes gives a more extended comment or even expands into description.

Usually, what I state as a fact can be relied upon as fact but, because I was not writing formal biography, I have not gone far beyond the obvious reference books, or the works of the writers themselves, and their letters to me where I had letters. On the whole also I have confined myself to the lives only in so far as they impinged on mine, since I do not claim to be writing more than recollections.

Even then, of course, there has had to be selection. I have not always said all that I knew. The dead may be presumed to be indifferent. The friends and enemies they have left behind are entitled to a decency of reticence which I would not willingly or wittingly transgress.

Memoirs as brief as these resemble the short story in that everything given must count, so that the whole may be a harmony. And I have been governed, intuitively more than consciously, by a principle of inclusion that takes as primary the personal relationship between my subject and me, and by my own conception of his character, what interested me about him, what brought us together, what I liked—or even loved—in him, what I thought to be flaws sometimes, even though flaws acceptable or at least tolerable to me, but especially those flaws which might help to explain why he did not become as a man or achieve as a writer all that he seemed at the time to have it in him to be or to create.

Only a very prodigal writer of fiction can afford to waste his effort and experience in direct autobiography. I am not prodigal, either by temperament or by wealth of vitality or by permissive circumstance. I have therefore tried to subdue my own egotism and keep my own role in these memoirs as subordinate as possible, intruding my presence only as far as it is necessary to account for a situation, explain a background, elicit an event, or reveal the kind of witness I take myself to be.

Yet sometimes the footprint in the clay is the only evidence for the light step that passed over it. And I am aware that, do what I might to the contrary, my own character and personality condition everything that I relate or describe. They, after all, determined in the first place that I should like this person rather than that, or that this or that person should like or dislike me; they determined also what sort of person I saw in the sense that we see and hear only what we have eyes to see and ears to hear. Moreover, because we are social animals and complete only in so far as we are members of one another, we are largely the creations of one another; and continuously created, since as individuals we are an abstraction having neither reality nor duration and, even as social beings, we are endlessly being modified, undergoing entropy, and being renewed, by our changing relations with one another. So that it is not only my character—what society has made of me—that determines how my friend appears to me but also his conception of my character and my response to that conception. He changes in the light of what he sees in me that he wishes to please or chasten and I change likewise. According to his view of me, his confidence or judgement, he will display to me some parts of himself that he cannot so readily display to another.

The variables are immensely complicated, then. Some facts, some aspects, of our identities are common to all, observed and observers, some fluctuate with the different moods and masks, presuppositions, premises, and prejudices of all those weaving their endless pattern in our dance of mayflies.

And we are all entomologists of ourselves and others. Gossip, talking behind people's backs, is a necessary ingredient of our social culture, indispensable to it and at its best one of the finest instruments of our civilized living. We all know that we are talked about but, provided that we are spared those candid friends so dreaded by George Canning, we are able to be unaware of it most of the time as we are, happily, unaware of death. We can gossip with enjoyment about others, serenely forgetful that they at the very same moment may be gossiping with equal enjoyment about us. For gossip is a necessary exercise: it is the practice of our skills in social perception, the daily do-it-yourself art by which we refine and sharpen our sensibilities, subtilize our knowledge of others, check our knowledge by the competing perceptions of our cronies, remind ourselves of the relativity of all human truth and the exhilarating improbabilities of behaviour. Through gossip we acquire the sense of others without which we fail as social beings and which is the *sine qua non* of charity. Gossip is the currency of the existence beyond ourselves which delivers us from narcissism and without which love is vain, no better than adolescent fantasy, where the love's object is not objective, does not exist except as our own projection, and the lover does not accept, does not even know, that all human beings are imperfect and that love or friendship which do not see and acknowledge and accept imperfection in others with the same large tolerance we reserve for our own defects do not deserve their names.

But gossip about the dead? Does not the proverb enjoin that their epitaphs should always be favourable? It may be so for the truly dead. It is certainly a way of ensuring that they do not come alive. No man rises from an efficiently whited sepulchre. But these people of whom I write are not dead; not wholly dead, at least, while their work is alive and they themselves are remembered. Foolishly, though we know that bronze itself is not immemorial but only a little less quickly perishable than flesh and that fame is less immemorial than bronze, we nonetheless strive for life after death, by a projection of that same autonomic drive that makes us pursue a larger life while we still breathe. Though our knowledge of lost cultures—where is Ozymandias now?— assures us that the immortality sought by conquerors and artists and the anonymous scratchers of graffiti is ephemeral and by the scale of infinity not of much more duration than the mortal life it seeks to prolong, we do have for as long as our own culture lasts the works these writers have left behind.

And the penalty of life is that we who love the works in which it still pulsates, however we may be adjured by the austere to trust the tale and not the teller, are drawn irresistibly to want knowledge of the people who produced them, just as the lover can never know too much of the beloved, or at least thinks he cannot. A little of that sort of knowledge is what I aim to provide in this book. But I do so in the wish, the certainty, that the knowledge is interesting only because the works exist, transcending the fallibilities and frailties of their producers. If it were not so, then I should have been better occupied in writing fiction, or nothing. And if anyone who reads these memoirs and then the writers whom I commemorate says to himself: 'But this man was full of weakness whereas his poem is not,' then I ask him to turn back to the poem and consider whether he does not see it with a fuller and fresher eye because he now has some idea of what had to be transcended in order that the poem should be created.

I had thought of arranging these pieces in the chronological order of the deaths with which each ends but have come to prefer the chronological order in which they were written. I am not sure why I wrote them in the order I did but I hope that I learnt as I went along a little more about what I was trying to do and that by preserving this order of composition I may be giving the collection a cumulative force and that the end will not diminish the beginning but instead will give it a fuller completion.

The pieces were written at various times over a period of about five years. Each was written as a unity, and intended to be capable of standing by itself. Reading the pieces again with a view to gathering them together, I have pondered whether I ought not to rewrite them wholly so as to make them uniform with one another in style, tone, and plan. I have decided that this would not be right. Preparing to write each of them I saturated myself at the time in the works, the letters of the man, recapitulating in my mind the period of my friendship with him, reviving my sense of his style and here and there, with a view to reinforcing subliminally my presentation of him, even allowing something of that style to murmur a message beneath my own. If I had rewritten them, something of the original spontaneity, the pressure and intensity of concentration, would have been bound to go; the individual would have been subordinated to the group and perhaps also to my more deliberate, critical, levelling self. And, once committed to such a subordination, I should have had to provide a setting, a sort of social history of literature in our times, and this would probably have been beyond my powers and in any case not possible in the time available to me. At least, however, I may have provided a grub's eye view of Worm Street, a toad's eye view of the harrow.

Eschewing major revision, then, I have had to countenance a number of repetitions. But the same scene with a different character in the foreground is not really the same scene, however closely one tries to cleave to the facts. Just as in a novel one can repeat a scene with different facets and emphases so as to display more variations of truth, that dancer with so many more veils than seven, so it has seemed to me that the same Soho pub, for example, was a stage for the adventures of Dylan Thomas very different from the stage where Julian Maclaren-Ross enacted his daily tragicomedy. And the Oxford where Joyce Cary and Enid Starkie based their adult lives, and where Louis MacNeice encountered and courted his first love, was a different Oxford for each of them.

Again, it may seem to the reader that the implied picture of a life and lives extending over some twenty years suggests that I spent these years entirely in the company of writers. In some ways, since I prefer the company of writers to that of authors (a distinction to which a publisher is inevitably in time reduced), I wish it had been so; but, of course, it was not. I saw these particular friends of mine at intervals only, and for long periods some of them I scarcely saw at all. One had many other lives to live among quite different friends and acquaintances and with one's own family; and the same was equally true for them.

Yet, for that part of me which is a writer, these particular friends were of essential importance in a way that other friends, however much cherished, were not. There have been times when I thought I might attempt to treat them in the manner of Plutarch, grading and comparing, if only to get their importance to me clearer. But I have preferred to treat each of them as unique. Why should I set against each other as novelists Joyce Cary and Julian Maclaren-Ross, two men whose characters grated against each other in life but neither of whom grated on me, two writers who tried to do wholly different things in fiction but things each in their different way acceptable? Or poets like Rodgers and MacNeice and Dylan Thomas, friends who delighted in one another and delighted in one another's poetry, accepting without begrudgement that they were writing poetry of different kinds but each trying ultimately for the only standard of true excellence, his best?

So I have presented each of them more or less in isolation, alone and separate, as the writer must be when he is writing, in much of his most important living, in his dying, and in what survives of him. It is a sumptuary restriction I impose on myself with some regret; for a full understanding of how they came to be what they were and write what they did really demands a larger canvas with room for the literary company they kept and its influence upon them. Into such a picture—not to speak of the living—would come other poets such as Roy Campbell, Norman Cameron, Bernard Spencer, W. H. Auden, and novelists and musicians and painters and raconteurs in infinite numbers. Even so one would be passing over those other friends like Shakespeare and Donne and Blake and the whole chrestomathy of poetry and art, Malraux's imaginary museum, which each man carried in his memory.

One generalization may perhaps be attempted, under the rubric of the 'social relevance' now modish; though, like much else so labelled, it is likely to be a truism rather than a truth. However total the commitment of the writer to his art, he cannot escape the difference that money makes to the way he lives his commitment. Of the people about whom I am writing only Joyce Cary and Enid Starkie had some sort of financial security. Even for them, in the beginning at least, it was frail. After his early retirement from the Colonial Service Cary's small private income was just adequate to support him and his family; even then it would hardly have sufficed without his wife's faith and courage in accepting sacrifice. He had to live austerely and frugally for years before success freed him from financial cares—too late for his wife to do more than taste the change.

Enid Starkie eventually found financial security, but the relative poverty of her family after her father's early death and her anxiety not to be a burden made her a cruel spartan to herself and left her with a habit of parsimony that survived the necessity by which it was occasioned. And the teaching by which she earned security was done with such neurotic conscientiousness that the books of her later life suffer from being written out of the remainder of energy rather than out of its fulness.

As for the others, MacNeice alone achieved a sort of security, having a permanent job at the BBC and the conscientiousness and power of punctilious application to go on holding it. Even then, only a man of the most stubborn and abundant creative energy, and an Ulster canniness in commitment, could have had enough will and vitality left over at the end of the day and of duty to write the poems that he wrote. And it could be argued that it was the job, the obligation he felt to it, that led to his untimely death.

W. R. Rodgers, again, made his living for a great part of his life from the BBC. He was scrupulous, however slow, in the discharge of his endless commitments—the excellent but ephemeral programmes carried through so brilliantly, the pioneering radio-portraits that survive still as classics, the often trivial tasks which he undertook to keep self and family alive and which left him so little time with which to build himself a monument in verse.

Maclaren-Ross was even less fortunate, misled by early success, unable to believe that society did not recognize it owed a living to its writers, and a good living at that; still more unwilling to accept that, instead, society expected its writers to pay tribute in taxes as if they were ordinary men. A man who burnt up money and burnt out himself in the pursuit of the opulence he thought he needed, he pursued the mirage of success in the films, became incapable of distinguishing between fact and fantasy, and so failed to make the transition from a promise to a prime. Instead, the promise became promises. His courage hypertrophied into arrogance and his integrity into uncompromising egotism. He wanted both to have his pride and drink it but, because his real gifts were those of a solitary, he could not earn a living at anything that involved being a member of a team or conforming to an office routine. So he was unable to use the BBC as a way of living, still less as a way of life. And the immense strain he put upon his own physique and fortitude, remarkable both, carried him off before the turning of luck on which he always counted could be put to the test.

The irony in the fate of Dylan Thomas, no compensation for its tragedy, was that security came only after he was in the safety of the vault. Fame he had in his lifetime but he was endlessly harassed by financial cares, all the worse because he knew they were often due to his own foolishness. For it is foolish in our time to try and live by being a poet, live like a man who is not a poet, have a wife and home and children, and yet give hours and years of time to the creation of poetry, with financial reward only a panic and belated afterthought. All praise to such men, however tiresome, badgering and bothering, unpunctual and unreliable, drunken, dilatory, and disaster-prone. They are our voices, the voices we cannot ourselves raise; and our senses, the senses that we starve; they are the interpreters of a world we are too meagre to experience directly for ourselves.

Itzik Manger was another such, a lyric poet who wandered this country for a decade of exile, writing and speaking a mother tongue known to few, the multitudes who once shared it having been destroyed by genocide. Kept alive in the dark years of his anguished maturity by the charity of others, his only security the love his transparent genius inspired even in those who could not understand him, he had to wait until his last lustrum, when his powers were almost spent, before there was welcome and a final refuge in Israel.

There are others from the past, soldiers and scholars, whom I might some day wish to try and celebrate also; but I mention them now only to indicate that there are parameters to these recollections which may not be immediately apparent: the world of learning with the piety towards the past which it teaches one to cherish; and the war which taught my generation and the one before us how sudden death is, how unjust in its election, how heedless of whether or not the lives it cuts off have been fulfilled.

My chief parameter, however, is that of art, since it is writers who most concern me now. And art, as their lives abundantly reveal, exacts suffering, beyond the common measure. For suffering is the hydrogen to that oxygen of living without which there is no flow, and it is to the breath of joy in the proportion of two parts to one. An ideal state would mean its extinction. But any other state inevitably provides the essential anguish of the poetry with the condition that the poet dies too soon, or if not the poet then his genius, exhausted or corrupted or atrophied or etiolated by the struggle. Such must be the fate of the artist in any polity we have known or are likely to know. If he has anything original and true to say it will be unwelcome to the ears of his time. Silence, exile, cunning maim what they are intended to shield. He will need luck, dedication on his own part and sacrifice on the part of others, and fanatical, irrational obstinacy. He will have to endure the temptation to believe that the failure of response in others is his own failure; and if and when they respond he will have to resist the acids of success and be content to live laborious days. His compensations are the work well done and the love of living and the delight of the various world.

These compensations my seven writers certainly had, though only three of them—Joyce Cary, Enid Starkie, and Itzik Manger —for something like the normal span. The first two, had they lived on, had work to do which would have been worth having, even if it did nothing to alter our present notions of their worth. Itzik Manger's last two or three years were years of illness and what he had to say may have been said—one cannot know. Julian Maclaren-Ross, always unpredictable in his phoenix-like power to re-create himself from disaster, might yet have written again by the standards of his early work had he been granted, improbably, the tranquil circumstances and the security in which to do it. And W. R. Rodgers was struck down by a mortal cancer years before one need have despaired of more fine poetry from him. At the time of Louis MacNeice's death we know from *The Burning Perch* that he was writing lyric verse of a tragic intensity unmatched in his former poetry. And it is hard to believe that Dylan Thomas would not have gone on to flash even brighter lightnings through the thunderheads that were always gathering about him.

All their lives were in this sense incomplete. But it is this finality of interruption that has made me feel able to write about them and made me feel in writing that I am contributing my funeral keen, my personal lament for the makers whom death has unmade.

ACKNOWLEDGEMENTS

Many friends, witnesses and survivors of time past, have helped me with these recollections. I did not always note their names or the particular service and I fear and greatly regret that this present attempt to recall the names of all those to whom I have been in some important way obliged is bound to be imperfect. But I believe—*crede experto*—that gratitude is possible even towards those whose names one has ungraciously forgotten and so I would like to put it in the forefront.

For help with the memoir of W. R. Rodgers I am particularly indebted to his widow, Marianne Rodgers, to his daughter, Harden, and to his old friend, the poet John Hewitt, whose lines in elegy of Rodgers are perhaps the finest memorial of him, other than that left by Rodgers himself.

To Hedli MacNeice I owe an old friendship which began the day I first met Louis and first met her, and much else, including at least one useful correction to the memoir included here. I am grateful also to Louis's sister, Lady Nicholson, and to his friends Francis Dillon and Anthony Thwaite who read the memoir in draft. And I would like to acknowledge also the close reading and encouraging criticism I received from Louis's one-time colleague and deeply cherished friend and mentor, Professor E. R. Dodds.

The memoir of Enid Starkie owes much to old friends of hers and mine who read it in various stages. I particularly wish to acknowledge the help of Dr. Robert Shackleton, her literary executor; Miss Peter Ady; Miss Jean Banister; Miss Audrey Beecham; Miss Joanna Richardson, her biographer; Dr Godfrey and Dr. Peter Lienhardt; and Professor Neville Rogers.

For help and encouragement with the memoir of Joyce Cary I am most grateful to his sons Sir Michael Cary and Tristram Cary and would like to take this opportunity of saluting their kindness and friendship over many years. I acknowledge also the help of

Mrs. Barbara Fisher who read a draft of the memoir but whose services to all those interested in the work and life of Joyce Cary go far beyond anything it would be appropriate or even possible to mention here.

Mrs. Margaret Taylor read an early draft of the memoir of Dylan Thomas and provided some helpful suggestions for excision. Many other old friends of Dylan's also read it in draft and I would especially wish to name Professor Reggie Smith, Professor Neville Rogers, and Miss Audrey Beecham.

The memoir of Itzik Manger owes a great deal to friends of his and mine and to others who helped out of love of Yiddish poetry. In particular, I want to thank his widow, Mrs. G. Manger; Joseph Leftwich; Mrs. Bil Costello; Mrs. Tamara Deutscher; Miss Margaret Waterhouse; Mr. N. S. Doniach; Professor Chaim S. Kazdan; Sir Isaiah Berlin; Professor C. H. Schmeruk; Mr. Asher Sarna; Professor Samuel Schoenbaum; and Mr. Meyer W. Weisgal.

To these names I would like to add those of others who have been helpful in the reconstruction of half-forgotten events or who have read drafts or otherwise assisted in ways that apply to more than one of these memoirs: Miss Martha McCulloch; Miss Nuala O'Faolain; Professor Beth Darlington; Professor Harriett Hawkins; Mr. John Willett; Professor Reggie Smith; Drs. Godfrey and Peter Lienhardt; Joel Carmichael; and my colleague and friend, Peter Sutcliffe.

Finally, there is the part played by my own family, not merely in reading and criticizing what I had written, but in creating and sustaining the ambience in which these and so many other friendships had their being and without which they would have been so much more anaemic and meagre. Here and there in these memoirs my wife and three daughters, Anna, Delia, and Brigid, appear as minor characters. In the life that lies behind the memoirs their role was stellar. And my wife's special role I signalize, with a terseness that does not do it justice, in the dedication to this book.

Oxford   D.M.D.
June 1974

Good Night, Julian, Everywhere

Julian Maclaren-Ross

1

*Good Night, Julian,
Everywhere*

JULIAN MACLAREN-ROSS
(1912-1964)

BLACKOUT, ration books, clothing coupons, spivs and
brackets, shortage of spirits and even of beer, black-market
restaurants and exiguous steaks, cigarettes hard to get and in
flimsy paper packets, the flying bomb and the V2 going bump in
the night, *Penguin New Writing*, *Horizon* and its Begging Bowl—
all these return half-credible when I think of the time I first came
to know Julian Maclaren-Ross.

Just before the fall of Florence, in the autumn of 1944, I had left
the New Zealand Division in Italy and come back to a staff job in
London. A few stories of mine had been published, my first novel
was in proof and I was writing another. Inevitably, I gravitated of
an evening to the Wheatsheaf, which I had frequented in the
Oxford vacations before the war. It was crowded now, compared
with what it had been. But the friends of my undergraduate days
were gone and I knew no one.

After so long among soldiers and my countrymen, I had become
a provincial again, pining for the society of writers but knowing
no way of breaking into their company. I waited, and drank
alone.

One evening I was sitting at a table in the corner, next to old
Mrs Stewart who drank Guinness and laboured over the cross-
words in the evening papers. She sat and wrestled with their

elementary problems, like an ant with a straw, but I had seen her reject furiously offers of help. Guinness she accepted.

Now one such Guinness was put in front of her. Looking up I saw Julian Maclaren-Ross. I had read *The Stuff to Give the Troops*, then lately published, stories of the army in the years before D Day and Julian's war with it. And I knew his name, face, and voice, all memorable, though I did not know the man himself. He was with a rather large man in a tweed jacket, yellow waistcoat, and corduroy trousers. Glass in hand, they stood above me talking.

Keidrych Rhys, as the other man turned out to be, became aware of my presence and began to stare, hostile. A stranger, in officer's uniform, I was reason for discomfort. He wanted to scratch and get rid of the itch. My New Zealand shoulder tabs provided the pretext.

I was invited to agree what a dirty game of rugger the All Blacks played. A notable, if exceptional, defeat by Wales at Cardiff was recalled with provocative satisfaction. Maclaren-Ross stood aloof, no rugger player and no nationalist. But clearly for him also my uniform, my major's crowns, my existence, were an offence.

Silence would have been dumb insolence, and my mild expostulation on behalf of my countrymen was no better. Keidrych's soft Welsh voice developed a note of menace. His leer was not civil, and contained no assent. I began to consider how, when the flashpoint came, I must upset the table against his thighs and get my blow in before he recovered his balance.

'But look. He can read,' Maclaren-Ross said. 'He's got a copy of *Penguin New Writing*.'

The tone was insolent, though cool. But I had no wish for a fight unless one were forced on me. 'It's got a short story of yours in it,' I said.

'You know my name?' A little mollified, he was wary. Admirers could be bores. And I myself felt a little guilty. My admiration was not whole-hearted. His army stories were brilliant. But the army they dealt with was not my army, his war was not my war.

'Perhaps you'll tell us your name, then,' he said.

I told him, keeping Keidrych in the corner of my eye.

'Didn't you write a story, "Under the Bridge", in *New Writing* Number Thirteen?'

The story was in fact mine. Mollified in my turn, I did not know yet how uncommon among writers was this memory for the precise particulars of what other writers had published.

'Why didn't you tell us you were a writer? We thought you were an officer. Have a drink.'

So it began, a friendship with Julian rather than an entry into the literary world. For he was already at feud with most of the habitués of the pub and of that world. To be a friend of his meant not being a friend of a good many other people. He was arrogant and exacting in company. He did not like to take his turn in conversation; or, rather, when he took his turn he did not let it go. To those who were not prepared to let him have the lion's share, in talk and attention, he seemed a pretentious bore. There were others, however, who managed to cohabit with him the narrow world of the Wheatsheaf, the Marquis of Granby, the Bricklayer's Arms, the Fitzroy, and the Highlander. Life became more diverting for acquaintance or friendship with its planets—Nina Hamnett, Dylan Thomas, Augustus John, the Lindsay brothers, Gerald Wilde. Tambimuttu came and went with his train, a comet rather than a star, black-rimmed fingernails gesturing, a wild dark and crafty eye, attendant girls and minor poets. To Julian, all these people were mere background for himself, whirl though they might as centres for their own worlds. He did not like rivals and preferred to keep his own court.

His irregular habits were as regular as being short of money allowed. Midday in the pub till closing time, a late lunch at the Scala restaurant in Charlotte Street, roast beef with as much fat as possible and lashings of horse-radish sauce. A stroll to look at the bookshops in Charing Cross Road and to buy Royalty, his special jumbo-sized American cigarettes. Opening time again at the Wheatsheaf till closing time. A hurried dash to the Highlander which closed half an hour later. Back to the Scala for supper and coffee. At midnight the tube home from Goodge Street, where a mad blonde known as the Goodge Street Whore lurked in ambush, convinced he was a homo and therefore a blackleg, and waiting to rave insults until the train bore us away.

My first acquaintance with a writer's life, even I could guess it wasn't typical, or at any rate not typical for writers who actually wrote. He had lately been working in some kind of Ministry of Information film unit and he was obsessed, I soon found, with films. At the drop of a hat he would become Eduardo Ciannelli or Sidney Greenstreet. *The Maltese Falcon* was a kind of paraclete. *Laura*, especially, was an infatuation. He identified with Waldo Lydecker and, although Waldo did not form his persona, he certainly reinforced it. I suspect that it was from Waldo's final quotation from Dowson, rather than direct from Dowson, that he got the title for his autobiographical volume, *The Weeping and the Laughter*. And if one got him off these, there was always the other reef to be driven on—the thriller. Dashiell Hammett, Chandler, Simenon, he had the glass key to them all. And all roads led to Hangover Square. *Jonathan Wild* was one of the few books he seemed to have read before Oscar Wilde. But in the twentieth century he seemed to have read everything and what he had read was immediately accessible to his memory. A favourite game was to challenge him for the title, characters, publisher, author, date of publication, of some obscure novel. A walking bibliography, he could always answer.

I learnt a lot from him, almost without knowing it. My own weakness in those days was the grand style. His company was therapeutic. It was he who pointed out to me that anecdotes of the war, which I used to tell and which I took to be no more than anecdotes, intent as I was on Tolstoy, were really short stories which needed writing. If it hadn't been for this I might never have written 'The General and the Nightingale'.

So each night we went our rounds and talked, the soldiers and the prostitutes bargaining and bickering on street corners, the pubs bulging, the occasional buzz-bomb crossing overhead with its flaring tail. One midnight we sat in the Scala, at a table under the window. In mid-sentence—Julian's, since his was usually the monologue—we found ourselves scrambling beneath the table. A second later table and ourselves were enveloped in the blackout blind, the broken window cascading round us. We lifted our shield and picked ourselves out of the shivered glass. The blackout was restored, the lights came on, we had more coffee.

Such intrusions of the rudely real were not common. Julian's life was more typically a routine which left his fancy free to elaborate its mosaic of plans for books and stories, his tales of the sins and derelictions of editors and publishers, schemes for raising money, fantasies about films he would one day write and produce, the life of Weidmann the Mass Murderer especially. Then there were the quarrels with landladies and taxi drivers—'Constable, take that man's number'—the injustices which pursued the artist, the endless and dynamic creation of his role of persecuted author at odds with all manner of slight, perfidy, and malignant misfortune.

At this time he was in high favour with the critics, even those he had insulted. His writing was in demand and he took pride in extorting the highest possible fee in cash and the speediest possible publication. He believed that an author should exact the largest possible advance on royalty; for that made the ignorant and indolent publisher print as many copies as he dared and really do his best to sell them. He used the telephone like a mortar, to lob his bombs right into the publisher's dugout, if the long-range barrage of letters was ineffective. If all else failed, there was always the frontal assault, and many an office knew him baleful in the anteroom.

At first I used to wonder when he managed to write, and marvelled at his prodigality in anecdote. He would tell the same story over and over again, its high points always a little more clearly focused, the dialogue cut finer and finer, the extravagances gaining authority from development in repetition. At a certain point, and after many tellings, it must all have crystallized. For then he would be in the pub one morning, the anecdote now a short story, written out in the most legible of minute scripts, ready to be printed without alteration, unless the crass compositor thought he had detected an error. In this matter of copy, he was a true professional, craftsman as well as artist: he loved not only to write well but the very tools of his trade, his treasured Parker fountain pen (always spoken of as 'the Hooded Terror'), his notebooks, his carefully drafted list of contents or synopsis, his titles as long pondered and tried on the tongue as the stories themselves.

He delighted in laughter, but even more in anger and drama. His talk was much of violence, though preferably at one remove. One evening I had to eject from the pub a drunk and troublesome Canadian soldier, who escaped a finishing blow and ran across the road. I came back from unsuccessful pursuit and was given by Julian a blow-for-blow playback of the brief encounter, as though I had not been a party to it—except for instructions on how I might have settled my man more effectively.

His invariable stick, gold-topped when it wasn't lost or in pawn, and then a silver-topped substitute, was for defence as well as ostentation. And sometimes needed: his dress courted derision from the drunken and the spiv. At a time when clothing shortage forced most civilians into a drab uniformity, Julian ransacked Charing Cross Road for garments more striking—a huge teddy-bear overcoat, a liver-coloured jacket perhaps and beige trousers. He could not afford custom-built cut but at least he would have the colour. His hair, too, was long in a way the army had made unfashionable, his carnation buttonhole renewed each day from a barrow was a provocation, and it was not only the Goodge Street Whore who took him for a queer and consequently fair game.

My impression is that physically he was timid but that his pride would not tolerate his timidity. He was proud of his height, a good six feet, and it was necessary to his fantasies of power that he should think of himself and be thought of as formidable. It was part of his conception of himself as dangerous dandy, one of an army of one, with a regimental tradition that went back to Beau Brummel, Disraeli, Oscar Wilde, and Aubrey Beardsley. There was a touch of D'Artagnan in his persona, too, perhaps from his boyhood in France, and of Cyrano de Bergerac. He must so dress and demean himself as to challenge the lightning, and so use his nervous courage as to conduct it. Hence many difficult situations which quick wit and tongue, an Ancient Mariner's eye, arrogant bearing, and sheer force of vitality usually resolved, himself unscathed and with further resources for anecdote, legend, or story.

There was an element of paranoia, also: a power of attracting trouble and animosity which his imagination could easily transmute into enmity and even persecution. His mind nourished itself on notions of conspiracy, of evil forces constantly gathering and plotting. Thus, life became more exciting and more dangerous and the excitement and the danger made breath sweeter and more interesting to draw. On this sense of being a sort of innocent Macbeth he drew for the great novel he was always planning, 'Night's Black Agents'. And it may have been because that vision was only a baseless fabric that he never came to write it. Though there were other reasons.

It did not at once become clear, at least to those I knew, but the end of the war was a disaster for many writers. While it went on there was a captive mass audience, mad for any distraction from the shabby daylight and the dismal dark, starved of theatre and sport and the hundred diversions which in peacetime enable the English to dispense with art. Peace dissolved this audience. For Julian it had a further consequence. The war, and especially his captivity by the army, had forced on him inescapable contacts with people at large and prevented him from living wholly in a world of his own creation. In response to it he had created for himself a persona, but between him and the endless variety and pressure of the outer life there had been a real relation, even if compulsory. The war had given him raw recruits for raw material, and rubbed his nose in the stuff of humanity. The war had made them conscripts of one another. Now his public had dispersed, leaving him a prisoner of his persona, an actor in an empty hall. And he had lost the wartime drama of the given. Till now, even for civilians, life and death, sudden love and its withdrawal, violent change which needed art only for its shaping and not for its invention, were always in the foreground, the conditions almost by which life was lived. The tensions for the writer were ready-made, the bizarre itself was real, the incredible commonplace.

Peace dissolved all that. The epic element was withdrawn, the presuppositions of tragedy receded to the normal poles of birth and death. Drama had to be sought out, reality had to be courted. But, bemused by early success, Julian no longer had to contend

with the Depression which before the war gave him the material
for his novel *Of Love and Hunger* (1947). He was condemned by
his egotism, as well as his honesty, to write about what he knew,
and now all he knew was the narrow ground of Fitzrovia. The
skill, the technique, were still his, and much else besides. But the
passion had to turn inwards, and lose its vital connection with
compassion.

This coincided with the loss of a public. Peace soon forgot its
wartime pledges. The illusions it fostered at first—money from
the films, television, new publishers—soon faded in the bank-
ruptcies of the publishers, the return of shoddiness to the films,
and the beckoning wealth was fairy gold. Soho itself began to
disperse. The dream business set up its headquarters elsewhere.
New talents appeared, new middlemen. There were new mergers
and takeovers, and Julian was somehow outside. When the writers
formed and clustered again it was about the knees of the BBC, in
the Stag's Head, in the Whore's Lament, in the George. And
Julian, in the Wheatsheaf, was asking querulously where everyone
had gone.

By then I was already three years removed to Oxford, to an
exacting job, other friends, other interests. It was no longer possible to postpone living, on the mock-heroic pretext that one
might soon be killed. Occasionally still I found my way to the
Wheatsheaf–Scala escalator. Julian still rode it daily, still lived the
same life of pen to mouth, its expedients more desperate. I had
very little money but was rich compared with him. As his difficulties were at least partly due to his determination to be an artist
or nothing, his debts were in a sense debts of honour. He had
refused to compromise. I had compromised and I felt guilty.
Besides, I liked him and had learnt from him. It was only right
that I should be good for an occasional loan.

I knew more about publishing now and was concerned for the
fix he was getting himself into. He had always only needed time,
security for a little while, in order to write 'Night's Black Agents'.
The synopsis had been written and rewritten. Even I by this time,
though I have now forgotten it, almost knew the plot by heart.
But he was hard up. The wartime magazines that had taken his

stories were all folding. He couldn't afford to write the book, must always be doing reviews and short pieces—always delivered to time and on the dot, as is the way with emergency chores, the provisional always claiming priority over the permanent, the ephemeral elbowing eternity out of the way. One's great novel is like a wife: she can wait, because she knows she is all-important.

And so many publishers came to know the synopsis of 'Night's Black Agents' by heart, too. To get money to get the time, Julian began to accept advances on royalty while the book was still unwritten. Worse, he got advances from many publishers for the same book, persuading himself that, because they had behaved badly to him by the stern canons he reserved for publishers, he could behave badly towards them. In the end, the book could not be written because no single publisher would have been able to put up the sum required to buy out the interest of all the others.

To escape the dilemma he decided to write his autobiography instead: it was not a novel and not mortgaged by advances. It would be in four volumes. Only one, *The Weeping and the Laughter* (1953), ever got written. Of the rest, only fragments were to appear in his lifetime, in the *London Magazine* most of them, and the posthumous collection of these.

What special reasons he gave for not carrying out the original plan I have now forgotten. No doubt they were the usual ones. And it is true that he lived under endless pressure to finish small things quickly to get money for the rent, for food, cigarettes, alcohol, and taxis. Yet by 1950 I had begun to suspect that there was some other block, some incompatibility between his capacities and his refusal to accept or create the conditions necessary to fulfil them, that prevented him from writing a major book.

Not that he was lazy. He was capable of prodigious stints of work when cornered and desperate. His liking for alcohol, and the unusually large quantities he was able to drink, did not seem to impair his stamina or his faculties. It was his habit to write at night. After spending the day in pubs and drinking clubs, he would return to his lair and write all night long, in that hand of unchanging neatness, with economy, clarity, and point. When things got desperate, and deadlines had to be met, he could work for days and nights at a stretch, without sleep or food or drink except coffee, though not without tobacco. One came to believe, in those later years, that it was only under stress that he could or would write at all; but the conditions of stress made it inevitable that he should write short pieces for immediate returns.

He had been writing 'middles' for the *Times Literary Supplement* on writers who interested him—Raymond Chandler, Dashiell Hammett, Eric Ambler, William Faulkner, P. G. Wodehouse— and in case it might bring him some money I suggested he might work these up into a book on modern novelists. The idea attracted him and he thought it might be given shape: as he put it in a letter to me, 'the connecting link being that they show characters in action rather than through introspection or psychological analysis'.

This was in the autumn of 1952 and to discuss it he made his first visit to Oxford and stayed with us. The project itself fell through. At this time he was much more interested in *The Weeping and the Laughter* and I thought myself that it was important he should write his own books rather than books about others. A subsidiary object of the visit was to seek advice—more for the pleasure of getting it and the pleasure of disputing it than from any intention of taking it—about the negotiations for his autobiography. In the end he extracted an advance of £150 for it, a large sum as it seemed to me but to him disappointing.

As £75 of this had to go to his landlady, the respite was short; but in January 1953 he began to review for the *Sunday Times* and also about that time he was writing TV film scripts for Norman Collins. By the summer he was broke again and applying for help from the Royal Literary Fund. I was one of the 'respectable persons' who testified to his being 'in want or distress'. The upshot was that his landlady was paid £100. He still owed £200, he wrote, but things looked more promising: Muggeridge's *Punch* and its literary editor, Anthony Powell, were taking parodies and short stories of his and paying well.

But money dissolved with Julian like snow in the hot hands of a child. He had a thermostatic device which ensured that the heat was always on. In the autumn of 1953 he was writing to me: 'I've been at it without respite for about five weeks and I have neither been down town during that time nor had a moment to write a letter, except a business one now and then. The weekend before last I worked sixty-two hours solidly without going to bed at all; last weekend for forty-eight hours without sleep.

'Nature of work? A lot of short stuff for *Punch*; two very long extracts from my second volume of autobiography for Spender's magazine *Encounter*; and the outlines for three reminiscences which I'm supposed to do for the Third Programme. The object of this? To collect as much money in a lump as possible and then be free to settle down to a longer piece of work: i.e. a novel. Nor will these pieces be wasted; for they are mostly autobiographical, and though they'll have to be radically recast, they're useful studies for Part One of my next volume (which I shan't write till all this stuff is printed or broadcast).'

He never did accumulate that lump sum, and the novel never got written. I seem to remember that it was still 'Night's Black Agents'.

During these later years I had seen him from time to time in the Mandrake Club in Soho, where the host was Boris, but my visits to London were more and more taken up with business and I went to the club less and less often. The generation I had known was for the most part dispersed, and so in a sense was I. Besides, though I did not mind the occasional blood transfusion of a loan or buying Julian a drink, I found it tiresome to be regarded as a sort of blood bank for casual friends of his who were more often than not neither amusing nor talented and who were tolerated by Julian himself for the only loan they could afford, their ears.

So I tended to see him only in the week-ends he stayed with us in Oxford when the breath of creditors was too hot down his neck. These visits my wife and I on the whole enjoyed—they were brief, he was comparatively free of care and at his most genial, and he went back to London about the time our stamina was giving out.

Towards the end of August 1954, however, he decided to make a permanent escape from London. The latest of his girl friends, and the only one I had liked since the very nice one who had been with him in the Wheatsheaf days, had left him. Worse, she had taken with her the cat, Rashomon. He had always had a girl but this was the first time he had had a cat. Rashomon had symbolized the hope of stability, a home in the floating world. The blow was crushing.

Now he was going to begin a new life in Oxford. Rather to our dismay, he found a room in our street, a few doors along from us. 'Dismay' perhaps needs explaining. In the first place, Julian was a possessive friend. In the most favourable circumstances it was difficult for him to believe one could value people he did not know or did not give himself time to like. Again, like many visitors to Oxford, he tended to react in a hostile way. I suppose Oxford is a specialized taste. Those who live in it develop their specialized habits and forms of reference. It is parochial. It ought to be provincial, yet it resists metropolitan patronage. The visitor from the great city, expecting to patronize, is nettled at the apparent complacency of people who care little for the intrigues and dramas and reputations of London, who gossip by a different set of Christian names, who wait politely until the grand stranger has dispensed his outside information and then go on with what really interests them and is gibberish to him. To a non-academic writer like Julian, who thinks in terms of what he conceives to be the literary great world, the circus of the university, so far from Piccadilly and so concerned with books and themes of a quite different order, can be at once boring and provoking.

Julian, moreover, had never paid lip service to the convention that requires one occasionally to make a show of listening to others. And it exasperated him that we had friends whose interests bored him but to whom we would listen, even though he himself was present. It was amusing, if painful, to watch his furious silence the night he first met John Wain. John had dropped in at the local and was full of his dealings with publishers over the novel he had lately finished, *Hurry On Down*. To Julian he was a frivolous interloper, not only in the pub but in the literary world. Why should this amateur, this whippersnapper Johnny-come-lately, this pampered don, be allowed to talk in front of a real writer, and especially about publishers?

Or, again, there was that difficult night at Joyce Cary's. Joyce,

himself the soul of good manners and kindness, found Julian a
bore and pretentious, but was willing to do him a good turn
because he was hard up, a fellow writer, and a friend of ours. So
he invited him along with us to meet a distinguished American
editor who was staying with him, a man who had known most
of the writers of the pre-war generation whom we admired and
who had been the friend and publisher of William Faulkner. The
result was catastrophe: Julian got into a fierce dispute with the
American by arrogantly asserting he was totally wrong about the
dates of the publication of Faulkner's novels. My efforts to point
out that both of them were right, one meaning the dates of
English publication and the other of publication in the United
States, went unheard. Joyce, who hated self-assertiveness, for once
abnegated his duties as host and withdrew from the room un-
noticed by the disputants. My wife eventually found him in the
basement, poring over his old bound volumes of *Punch*. She
assured him that the quarrel was over and brought him back. It
was over in the sense that the rivals had settled for a silence of
intense mutual dislike. We took Julian away as soon as we decently
could, and as we walked home he exulted in his demolition of
yet another impudent American impostor while we ruefully
reflected that a promising ally in his attempts to get publication
in America had been alienated for ever.

At this period, and indeed throughout his life, Julian alternated
brief spells of affluence with long stretches of no money at all.
During the bad times he came to the local pretty regularly. The
rest of us all drank beer but at this time he drank Moussec—
usually corrupted in those days to 'Dr. Moussadek' and eventually
to 'The Doctor'. This poor man's champagne cost half-a-crown
a time, more than twice the then price of a pint. When, as often,
he couldn't buy a round himself, this could be irritating for those
who did pay, none of them very affluent. The only way round
the problem was to lend him a pound or two and I was often
hard up myself. But he was touchy whenever he needed to touch
and so great caution was called for. The best method of compen-
sating him for having had to borrow was to encourage him to a
monologue about films, or thrillers, the iniquities of publishers,

or life in the army. When this was not possible, he would sit glaring silently at the company.

If things got really desperate, he would stay at home and work himself into utter exhaustion, sustained only by his favourite pill, 'the green bomb', which he would explain had the useful property of being 'good for rage' and simultaneously 'pepping you up and calming you down'. When he urged it on me as a specific for my own hypochondria I found it excessive: I talked all night and all next day, and then lapsed into a profounder gloom than ever before.

Towards the end of one of these Balzacian working spells, notes carried by his aged landlord and inscribed in capitals 'Private and Personal: By Hand' would slip through our letter-box. Sometimes they were indignant. He had been let down yet again by other people's selfish frailty, usually mine. 'I arrive at the Victoria last night at 9, having bolted my dinner in order to be in time, only to be told by Winnie—at 9.30—that you had "retired to bed": an explanation which seemed not only inadequate but ironical to a man who'd been nearly two days without sleep. I can't help feeling it might have been more thoughtful to have telephoned either the Royal Oxford or the Victoria and told me that a subsequent appointment with Morpheus prevented you from being there.'

This note was written after he had received a cheque. Whenever this happened, like the poet Richard Savage when he got his pension, Julian would go off by himself, usually to the Royal Oxford, and eat an enormous meal, with wine, cigars, and copious brandy, and thereafter be ready for company. It seemed outrageous that his friends, weaker brethren, should not be available to drink with him and listen while he described a new treatment for the film which was going to make his fortune as soon as he had found a discriminating backer.

The regimen of solitary large-scale dinners, followed by all-night talk with anyone who would listen, he regarded as merited solace for the periods of privation. It was useless to point out that the money would soon be gone and that the flush period would inevitably be followed by privation for consequence and sequel;

and quite out of the question even to hint that repayment of former loans might bear at least a low priority before the time for new ones began. When that film was made all loans would be repaid, and more than paid. For Julian there were two kinds of credit. On one, the one you got from friends, landladies, and the like, you could draw for only limited amounts. On the other, the credit to which you were entitled for your putative generosity, there was no limit.

So the money ran quickly out. Then the notes would take on their pathetic strain, the plea from the garrison abandoned and beleaguered. Appeals for books, cigarettes, food, would be carried sadly by the landlord and drop through the letter-box. My wife would load up her bicycle basket and wheel it to the rescue. At such times, yellow, gaunt, and desperate as he was with exhaustion, hunger, hangover, piles, anxiety, but never remorse, she always found him considerate and courteous. Not that his proud spirit was broken. No, but in his bare bedsitter she was his guest. And it was not altogether his fault that the only times he had a guest were when it was someone on an errand of mercy.

Kindness, of course, even in the best of women, has its backlash. And my wife used to get furious that he would spend in a day or two sums that would have been enough to keep our own household of a basic five going for a fortnight; that when his money ran out he would again be our responsibility; and that his feasts never included those who fed him when he was broke. For this last I was myself grateful. My particular Oxford problem was how to escape other people's hospitality and have a frugal meal alone.

Solitude, always hard to come by, was almost impossible to achieve with Julian for neighbour. On his way back from his blowouts or indeed at any time, if he saw a light in our window, he would call. Since his habits were nocturnal and he liked, as most of us do, to put off as long as possible the moment when the desk and the blank piece of paper must be confronted, he was happy to sit and drink whisky as long as our stamina and the bottle lasted. In mellow mood he was as good company as I have met, given a willingness to listen. But our positions were not the

same. My work had to be done by day and at regular hours. And
the time was almost past when I could sit up most of the night
and do an efficient day's work afterwards.

So it is with a smile of wry recognition that I read in Johnson's
Life of Savage:

He was sometimes so far compassionated by those who knew both his
merit and distresses, that they received him into their families, but they
soon discovered him to be a very incommodious inmate; for, being
always accustomed to an irregular manner of life, he could not confine
himself to any stated hours, or pay any regard to the rules of a family,
but would prolong his conversation till midnight, without considering
that business might require his friend's application in the morning;... it
was therefore impossible to pay him any distinction without the entire
subversion of all œconomy in the family, a kind of establishment
which, wherever he went, he always appeared ambitious to overthrow.

There were times, too, when the constant strain of Julian's life
made his pride very sensitive, he would construe some jest as an
insult, and withdraw in a dudgeon. The next day's note would as
like as not contain a challenge to a duel. I remember one such, on
a Monday to make matters worse, written no doubt as I was
getting up and he was going to bed. Guessing what was inside the
familiar envelope, and with a heavy day of meetings ahead, I put
off opening it until some time when I might feel better. I forgot
about the note and days passed. Julian had not turned up at the
local since, and I assumed he was working or had gone to London.
When eventually I brought myself to read the note I was dis-
mayed. It was a severe and in many ways accurate and acute
indictment of my character, going back as far as 1944—Julian's
remarkable memory extended especially to fancied slights—to
evince horrible instances of my insensitivity, ingratitude, selfishness, and generally coarse 'colonial' behaviour. Although too
much the prosecution's case, it was so feelingly and skilfully
written, so beautifully directed to my weak spots, that even after
all these years I am reluctant to read it again.

But the more usual formula was a tight-lipped and brief challenge, offering me swords or pistols. I regarded this as all nonsense
but, so powerful was Julian's gift for dragging even an exceptionally

sceptical bourgeois into his own fantasy world, I was never quite sure whether I ought not to accept. I would manage to suppress these misgivings, though, and would carry on with my usual routine. Julian would keep out of our normal orbit for a day or two, while he waited for my second to call. In the end patience or money would fail him, and he would compromise with strict punctilio and turn up at the pub. He would ignore my presence in a studied fashion and stand at the bar by himself with a drink, emanating menace, and waiting for me to do whatever the code demanded.

After a while, when it became clear I couldn't read the code, and he felt the atmosphere of the pub diluting the emanation, he would cross over to my table and stare at me through the dark mirror-glasses he had maddeningly taken to affecting. At length he would say, 'Did you receive a communication from me?' 'Yes.' 'Are you going to do anything about it?' 'No.' A long silence in which he would be trying to impose his will upon me after the manner of some admired film actor. Then I would say, 'Have a drink?' He would graciously accept, not without some relief, I suspect, at another anti-climax. I would buy him a 'Doctor' and peace would be restored.

I could not have been wholly despicable, in spite of my crimes. For once when he was in London for a day or two, he picked up in the Mandrake a report that I was dead. The telephone rang at home. My wife answered and Julian's voice asked in sepulchral solicitude how she was. She replied with unsuitable briskness and asked how he was. 'Don't let's talk about me,' he said, 'let's talk about Dan.' So unlikely a proposal soon elicited the truth. As Julian, like most of the old Soho, always relied on someone else to tell him what was in the papers, he had heard the story from someone who had heard it from someone who had read *The Times*'s obituary of an aged Irish senator with the same name as myself. But my wife always held it to Julian's credit that at least once he had been really concerned for someone else.

Death is one of the few situations where it is not easy for one of the living to grab the lead role. But there were other recurring situations where Julian could make concessions. In the eternal triangle of which, in the army, the Officer Commanding, the Sergeant Major, and the man on a charge are the dramatis personae, who represent in the more universal fabric God, Society, and erring humanity, Julian was often content with the minor part of Orderly Room Corporal, or Recording Angel. This was his best role, the one best suited to him as writer. But the actor in him, too often ham, made him long to play God or the villain, or victim.

Once, between Saturday opening times, he and I and Nina Hamnett left the Wheatsheaf by taxi for some Chelsea cinema where *The Lost Weekend* was on. It was a testing experience and my bravado at least was shaken. Afterwards, Nina had to be administered a stiff rum before she was strong enough to wait for a taxi in which to return to the Wheatsheaf. Julian, however, had found a skilful and satisfactory way of remaining unscathed. Instead of identifying with the alcoholic writer he simply became Bim, the male nurse in the alcoholic ward of the hospital. And Bim he remained for the rest of that night's wanderings, recalling with ever-increasing vividness and pleasure the imaginary mouse which had terrified the alcoholic's delirium and caused Bim such agreeable chuckles.

The recollection in dramatic monologue and faithful detail of such incidents as this made Julian at his best very good company. But towards the end of his Oxford period that best was passing. He had persuaded himself that he was in love with an utterly inaccessible woman. I had never met her—he himself could not have met her often—but I knew enough about her to know that she would never have reciprocated his infatuation even if she had been aware of it. And circumstances made it impossible for him to see her whenever she made brief visits to London from abroad. So our sessions after the pubs closed became almost unendurably embarrassing and boring. Hours of talk were devoted to minute analysis of her character, impossible plans for her subjugation, and the interpretation of signs and portents perceptible only to the frenzied fancy of Julian himself.

In desperation, I devised a defence. We had a lively kitten which loved jumping for a bit of string tied to the end of a child's fishing-rod. By so timing the kitten's jumps as to make each one an unwelcome caesura in Julian's sentences, I could eventually disrupt his monologue and exasperate him to the point where he would go off to his bedsitter and brood alone over his lamia.

That year, 1955, was a hard one for him and in some ways I think it was fatal to his talent. His obsession with the inaccessible girl seemed to mutate the quality of his imagination. In the end it drew him back to London, like a guerrilla returning from his hide-out in the *maquis*, and from now on he managed, mainly through large-hearted producers like Reggie Smith, who bore with him for the sake of his abilities, to make a precarious living writing thrillers for the BBC. He got married, though not to the lost lamia, and he had a son. He frequented the BBC pubs but I saw little of him. His interests were less than ever mine, I was embarrassed by my lack of sympathy for what he was writing, and there is always a strain in a friendship which has to be sustained by irrecoverable loans.

Besides, the friends whose company I nowadays found congenial, Louis MacNeice, Bertie Rodgers, René Cutforth, and others, shunned him as a ruthless bore; and the difficulty of meeting him and them in the same places at the same time became too much. In any case, I was now too busy, too tired and enmeshed in my own frustrations, to afford the unnatural concentration his egotism required and to pass whole days in pubs and afternoon clubs.

Nor could my wife help. For he had dedicated to her his *roman à clef*, *Until the Day She Dies*, in recognition of her support during the time of his hopeless passion. She found it intolerably bad, was unable to write and thank him for the dedication, and so had to avoid all risk of meeting him face to face.

So the friendship died away. He published two or three more books: a collection of *Punch* articles, two thrillers—one of them *Until the Day She Dies*, and another still worse. He was now, bizarre to the end, using a publisher in the Isle of Man, perhaps because, like Dylan Thomas, he was at last being hunted down by the Inland Revenue. I could no longer recognize in the work the writer I had admired, still less the writer I had hoped he would become. Only at the last something of the old quality flared up again in the reminiscences he wrote for the *London Magazine*. And when these were eventually published in the posthumous *Memoirs of the Forties* (1965), the torso of the book he had intended, I felt relief as well as regret that debt-collector death had dunned him too soon for him to be able to make the only repayment any of us really wanted, a finished book. For, when he died of a sudden heart attack in 1964, he had not written, as he had planned to do, about his 'Oxford period', the negative of what his photographic eye had registered of me was never to be developed, and I had escaped what would have been a painful exposure.

As Johnson said of Savage, another major talent of minor accomplishment, 'Those are no proper judges of his conduct who have slumbered away their time on the down of plenty, nor will any wise man presume to say, "Had I been in Savage's condition, I should have lived or written better than Savage".' And my own mind goes back to a Saturday afternoon in Oxford, years ago, when I had fled from his demanding monologue to my own down of plenty and woke in distress from my slumber to hear a voice saying, 'Good night, Julian, everywhere'. My mind cleared and I realized thankfully that the voice on the wireless was announcing the end of Children's Hour and not proclaiming the onset of Julian's ubiquity. But I hear the words now in my mind as a premature farewell.

At the End of his Whether

W. R. Rodgers

2

At the End of his Whether

W. R. RODGERS
(1909-1969)

IN 1970 in Dublin I found myself bailed up in the Bailey and agreeing to subscribe to a fund for restoring a Presbyterian church, and in Ulster at that. Me, brought up a Catholic by Irish parents from Galway and Cork—people for whom the North meant, not our New Zealand north (a hot, soft place), but the Black North Ulster, full of Black Protestants and bigoted Orangemen. It was the oldest Presbyterian church in Ireland, this one, at Loughgall in Armagh. But what if it was? What was that to me, a defaulter from a Church far older? The people who had prayed first at Loughgall were my ancestors, Catholic. The people praying there now, if Protestants could pray, were planted supplanters.

Was too much Guinness the explanation, then, or the sheer paradox of the thing? Or the great brown eyes, those of her father dead not long since, that Harden Rodgers turned on me? Something of that, yes; but more the story told with her and his wry smile, of how the pulpit in Loughgall was so high that, on those Sundays when Saturday had been the night before, Bertie—as even that staid parish knew its pastor—could stoop in a pause of his preaching, some cautiously contrived caesura, and retch gently, invisible to his devout and Sunday-sombre flock.

I tried then to remember whether I had met him or his legend first. In my memory it seemed to be the legend. Ulstermen who

had known him in those years of his ministry—1934 to 1946—
recalled life then in Bertie's house as a sort of poem, one of his
own poems. There was always sun or moonlight on apple blossom,
endless talk of life and death in the small big house full of books
and the small hours that never grew smaller, and a gay drift of
laughing girls flitting innocently carnal through the orchard. And
somewhere at the heart of it all would be Bertie, smoking his
eschatological pipe, nodding a compassionate head to the saint
and sinner in others and himself, anticipating indiscretion, con-
fession, disclosure, revelation, with the omniscience of his calm
'I know, I know'.

He was a great reader of the earlier English poets in those days,
trying to sidestep the rancorous antinomies of Ulster, and perhaps
he was hoping to create a parochial idyll and idol of Herrick. At
the least he would have been young enough and sanguine to think
with the roadmender who once answered an inquiry after his
health: 'God is good; and the devil isn't bad, thank God.'

This picture that his old friends called up was certainly not the
Black North, or the Presbyterian minister, that I had been prepared for. And it may be that the grimmer vision was more
typical than Bertie's legend, though I can doubt this as I don't
doubt those girls, the talk, the laughter, and the apple blossom.
For these fit more easily with the man I later came to know.

It was some time in 1948 that we first met. Two years had
passed since my transition from the New Zealand Division to the
Clarendon Press—hardly more than a change of unit, it sometimes seemed—and I had published a book or two of my own.
Bertie's *Awake, and Other Poems* had been published in 1941 when
I was elsewhere but people still remembered it and thought well
of it. Louis MacNeice, I gathered, had brought him over to
London at the end of the war and Laurence Gilliam had given
him a job in Features at the BBC. His wife Marie, a psychiatrist,
was working in a clinic in Edinburgh and Bertie was living with
friends in Wapping. I assumed he was whatever might be the
Presbyterian equivalent of a 'spoiled priest'.

We would have met in a pub somewhere, through friends. Not
Soho, probably—the tide of literary life had already ebbed from

there. It might have been the Lamb in Lamb's Conduit Street. Bloomsbury had only just begun to succumb to the arrogance of modern architects and the fungoid University. There was still a neighbourhood in Mecklenburgh Square and the streets round about. More probably, though, we met in the Stag's Head near the BBC where lunchtimes lasted through opening hours and where it was hard to distinguish poets from producers, since the roles were often doubled and neither would have been altogether embarrassed at being taken for the other, in those days before the Fall, before radio was relegated to the Age of Steam and the world became a global suburb.

Meeting Bertie for the first time, I remember sensing in him the decent pride and reserve of 'your quiet man' but it was not a glaçis that a stranger had to cross, as it was with Louis. The brown eyes were large, luminous, nocturnal like a lemur's. There were laughter wrinkles about them, though down-turning like the corners of the mouth, and so suggesting irony and wryness, the afterthoughts felt simultaneously with the gaiety they would succeed to, the bone of bitterness that is beneath and supports the ripple of Irish laughter. His voice was low and pleasant and the nuances intertwined in it like the colours in the Irish tweed he usually wore. There was a calm in him, like that of someone who was as much a witness as a doer. His dignity was that of a man who respected all men, and himself among them, not like the irritable dignity of teachers, or N.C.O.s, or spinsters in public life—people who fear that their authority is greater than their presence and must be continually reasserted. So, though you felt in him a passionate man, he moved calmly through other people's contentions and animosities and neither attracted nor emanated truculence.

Not long after we met I conceived a plan for a book—destined not to be published—which was to be called 'The Character of Ireland'. The editors I wanted were Bertie himself, and Louis MacNeice. This project was to become, as things turned out, the threat—I can hardly say rosary, and worry-beads would imply comfort—that would twine through what was left of their lives and perhaps what is left of mine.

Early in 1949 I went over to Belfast and Dublin, my first

visit since the war. Bertie had armed me with introductions and I saw Belfast through his eyes and those of his friends—Sam Hanna Bell, John Hewitt, George and Mercy McCann, James Boyce, John Stewart, and others. It was a more humane and friendly city than I would otherwise have seen, mediated through these men in Kelly's Wine Vaults, and many another pub with snug cubicles still haunted by Wolfe Tone. And in Dublin, too, I met his skein of friends, in the Pearl Bar where Smyllie of the *Irish Times* presided and in the Gresham Hotel where Peadar O'Donnell drank coffee and gave whisky to his friends. This too, the Dublin of Austin Clarke, Donagh MacDonagh, Paddy Kavanagh, Theo Moody, Ben Kiely, was a Dublin—or Dublins—it would have taken me a long time to find without Bertie's help, a place where every man had a self of his own which at one time or another he had permitted Bertie to see. For, if in a sense he had created the Belfast he showed me, he had himself in a sense been recreated by Dublin.

Domiciled in London now, he was, like a true expatriate, intensely preoccupied with the country—the two countries—he had left. These were the years when he was doing his best work for the BBC, the series of mosaic portraits made after the formula he himself originated of Irish writers—AE, Yeats, Joyce, the great men of Ireland in our time. It was natural, then, that the book I suggested should attract him. Plans went forward rapidly at first, reticulating and ramifying like a page from the Book of Kells. Conferences with him and Louis were frequent and agreeable, though seldom exactly according to arrangements. I recall a day in June 1949 when I cleared my desk of all appointments so as to devote all my time to my two editors. I had yet to learn that for Bertie 'Journeys are always curly'. The afternoon passed and they didn't come. It was after nine that evening when the telephone at home hooked me from the deep water of my study, where I was working on a book about the battle of Crete. Bertie's voice, full of whisky and placation, reported himself and Louis and Dylan Thomas bogged down at the George in Oxford. Would I join them?

No more work was done that night. The George foreclosing,

the conference that was not a conference adjourned to my house. It was early morning when I retired to bed and my two editors set off in high spirits to look at Oxford empty in the summer dawn and to visit Ernest Stahl. Dylan had capitulated an hour or two earlier and been put to bed in our attic. He awoke to learn over a lunchtime pint that they had been stopped by police who wanted to know what Louis had in his rucksack. 'But didn't you tell him, Louis, that you never travelled with anything but a change of verse and a clean pair of rhymes?'

The plan formed, the authors chosen and persuaded to promise performance, we settled down to wait for the articles. Louis went off to Athens for the British Council, and nothing much happened until he came back at the beginning of 1952. There was some question of whether they had been paid the expenses of the visit to Oxford three years before. In reply to my apology, Bertie wrote: 'You say "You will remember we discussed"—I don't remember. Not "in vino veritas", but "in risu veritas". I remembered only that I wished to see you, was intent on seeing you, and did see you. The other kind of money, with us Irish people, is something to forget with. And may I be allowed to forget what I said? And will you be forgetful enough to allow? I should be grateful.'

The airy dismissal of money was an agreeable and polite flourish only, not meant to take me in or himself either. We knew well enough even then, when he was regularly employed, that he was never likely to have, would not expect or want to have, 'the other kind of money' or any kind of money in the quantities you needed if you were ever to forget about it for long. Indeed, by the end of the following year, the hard fact could not be escaped. His first wife was dead. He had got married again, to Marianne, the former wife of Laurence Gilliam, and had become a free lance— was there ever a lance that was free, except in the sense of unemployed?—and he was at the end of his tether. He had to take a job with an advertising agency. The only slogan of his that I can recall was invented for some detergent or domestic cleanser: 'Is your Father a Mother or your Mother a Feather?' I do not think it was considered suitable, or that his services were long retained.

Meanwhile, 'The Character of Ireland' was not coming forward as well as it might. The reliable had sent in their articles, the others not. Threats and cajolery issued from the two editors. From time to time one or other of them would track down the recalcitrant in London, Belfast, or Dublin. But the subsequent discussion would normally take place in a pub, reproach would dissolve in jest or be so muffled and roundabout that it wasn't even perceived, and if the talk adverted again to its original purpose the reproach would be tainted and weakened by a feeling of discourtesy. Promises would be made by the laggard, as a concession to his host's discomfort and not as of right. And, as Dr. Johnson remarks, authors' promises are as readily forgotten as lovers' vows.

Nor were the editors able to cite example from themselves. The plan at this stage was that they should each write a poem for the book. In September 1952, Bertie had written and explained: 'In a moment of insight (or drink) I therefore suggested that Louis and I should devote the middle and hinging pages of the book to a pastoral hammer-and-tongs give-and-take on Partition, in which we might, as uncouth shepherds, say all the outrageous things which nobody dare put in urbane prose: Ireland forgives anything in poetry. Louis, I'm glad, likes the idea.'

For them as procrastinating poets the idea had an obvious advantage: they need not write until the other articles were in. As editors it gave them the consolation that the delays of others meant all the more time for them to meditate. So they shuttled and shuffled, sometimes alternately and sometimes together, between England and Ireland, sometimes on business for the BBC, sometimes for family reasons, and sometimes for our book; but basically because, though England kept them, Ireland drew them. The one country gave them a living; the other, life.

Once they returned with a tale of a railway crossing they had come to and found half-closed, somewhere in the west of Ireland. They eventually found the crossing-keeper in a pub not far away. 'But why did you leave the gate half-open?' Louis asked. 'Well, you see, sir, I was half-expecting a train.'

There were times when I felt that they themselves were only

half-expecting and I myself began to stop expecting at all. Year followed year and I tried every exhortation. Sometimes cash seemed the most likely stimulus. As one contributor, Conor Cruise O'Brien, put it: 'We Irish are, as you know, a deeply spiritual people, and the slower we are paid the more spiritual we get.' And Jim Phelan, by that standard the least spiritual since the fastest and most exigent of our contributors, followed up his article on tinkers by driving his gypsy caravan to Oxford and appearing in the office to collect his fee.

But there was always some new delay, vexatious and redoubtable. Someone's pseudonym was leaked and he had to withdraw his indiscretion, leaving us to find a substitute. Another was in the Government and decided he couldn't risk saying what he now thought ought to be said. Dylan Thomas died and Louis, as a literary executor, was deep in new responsibilities. Some contributors ratted, repented, and ratted again. When my letters became fierce instead of plaintive, one or other of the editors would arrive in Oxford to placate or reassure or to wrap me up in a night-long cocoon of good but bemusing talk that made reproach impossible. They usually took away and left behind a hangover, sometimes something else. Hence a worried note from Bertie in 1955: 'Have you seen in your office or at home, a little rounded metal tobacco-box, part of my pocket penates which I sadly miss?'

In June the next year Bertie came down for Auden's Inaugural Lecture as Professor of Poetry. He was tenacious in the ceremonial of friendship. David Cecil gave a party afterwards. Over in a corner of the room, where the drinks were, I can still see Bertie and Auden, each filling his glass in turn, and the heads going up as the drinks go down, tongues in full spate and laughter. After such an evening as this, we would usually go back to my house, where Bertie would be staying. As the whisky grew lower in the bottle, his voice would grow lower also. Craning to hear what he was saying, I would marvel half-resentfully at the skill of his monologue. To have any hope of getting an aria of your own, you would have to listen intently to try and find a gap where you might break in. So he started with the advantage of your attention. But there wouldn't be a gap. He used Scheherazade's

technique of the unended anecdote, like unclosed parentheses, so
that you could never cut him off.

Anecdote was the staple of his conversation at such times. He
mistrusted the abstractness of pure argument, its tendency to
polarize; he did not like talk to have a border, its North and
South. The advantage of a story was that the individual had flesh
on it, was unique; and, since somewhere in his recesses there still
seethed a preacher, the anecdote for him still carried elements of
the parable.

Thus he would tell a cherished tale of a parishioner rebuked for
some transgression who had replied: 'Never mind, your reverence,
the devil'll never light a whin-bush at your backside for my mis-
takes.' And he would smile and pull on his pipe and leave you to
draw the moral and to infer also, if you liked, that the parishioner
knew, or Bertie thought he knew, that the shepherd was one of
his own black sheep. Black sheep or not, it was clear that his
affection for the people of his parish was partly a reflection of their
fondness for him.

Or, to illustrate the love-hate between North and South, he
would recall the man challenged at the Border. 'Friend or foe?'
No reply and your man comes on, boots loud in the dark. 'Friend
or foe? Answer or I fire.' 'Foe.' 'Pass, foe.'

But in the end the soliloquy of that blackthorn mind would pass
to reverie. His low, withdrawn mumble would be less and less
audible, or comprehensible, the monologue totally interior. But
if his host, thinking of bed, pressed him too hard for his meaning,
the sharp reprimand could still flash from the crepuscular, 'If you
were as drunk as I am you'd know what I was talking about.'
For, behind the obscure double turnings of his talk at such times,
there was still a thread of theme, and he was still pursuing, and
being pursued:

> A tether that held me to the hare
> Here, there, and everywhere.

We were in 1956 now, and on the last day of August, Bertie
reported: 'I have started my Epilogue, meaning it to be a kind of
requiem or "wake" for the dead of Ireland; and what else was

Ireland ever, but her dead?' For the original plan for a central
verse dialogue had changed and the plan now was that Louis
should write a verse prologue and Bertie an epilogue. Bertie's
claim to have begun writing was to encourage me to produce
some expenses for his visit to Ireland, planned for September,
'first making sure that the foxes are at home'.

After he came back he was much preoccupied with tapes that
he had accumulated, then and over the years, of his talks with the
great Irish survivors. If I would co-operate, with money, and let
him have a session with Peadar O'Donnell, 'I'd get you the best
stuff that ever was got under the Irish lamps.' And there was
Richard Best he had recorded and many another.

But there was still no finished book and in March 1957 I evidently had to be reassured once more and thanked for I have forgotten what favour. 'And may I say, after all my undeserving,
that the world whittles itself down finely to a few persons who
matter to me, and you are one of the Gideon's army. Or, may I
put it another way, and extend—though not extenuate—the statement and say primitively that you bring me luck? I arrive here to
find that the waiting letters largely resolve my immediate problem. I'm a problem, of course, that will find its answer on its
death-bed (I'm thinking of patenting an elastic bed in order to
prolong life). Notice my commas and fullstops: they are very
careful ones: they have to be. "Young man," said AE to Joyce
who undergraduately brought his poems, written on purple paper
—purple birds of passage—for AE to give an opinion on,
"Young man, you have not enough chaos in you to be a poet."
Only an Ulsterman, like AE, would ever know the importance
of having a predestined chaos. "We don't want order," said
Harry Brogan (the Abbey actor, the only one) to me . . . "We
don't want order. And we don't want disorder. What we want is
orderly disorder. I don't know," says he (describing a figure of
eight on the table with his wet pint of stout), "how it adds up.
But it does."

'Let's now get down to business. (Oh, before I leave it, a story
about Brogan. Kavanagh said to me lately that lately Brogan said
to him in a moment of midnight confidence—"Seumas, my

mother was a corpse-washer in Dublin, and once she took me
with her to help turn over a big woman of twenty-two stone. I
was a very impressionable age, Seumas, I was only eight at the
time, and things like that could turn you against things. But
thanks to God, Seumas, I'm married and have a very nice family.")

'You and me have a lot to be thankful for. But now to business . . .

'One last thing:—I read to you last night, Richard Best talking
about Bergin. Sarah Purser painted Bergin's portrait and asked
me round to see it. I remember Douglas Hyde was there, and
Hyde, when the portrait was hoisted on the easel, said, "Who is
it? Who is it?" And she looked very crestfallen. "Is it a judge?"
"Yes," I said, "it's the judge of us all. It's Bergin."

'And now—I shall write, myself—would you, on the heels of
last night, say a good word for me to the judge of Us All?'

The years passed. Most of the articles had come in, some of
them had gone out again, and some had come back, revised.
Others, meanwhile, needed to go out again, having gone out of
date. But we seemed in sight of the end, except for Louis's prologue and Bertie's epilogue. Louis was at length persuaded to
commit himself to a date. He did not like committing, especially
himself, because he kept his word more than most. He did so now
and in 1958 it was delivered. Bertie's poem was promised for the
Christmas of 1960. Christmas came but not the epilogue. Contributors grew restless again, clamouring to be paid or published.
Some had already gone home and taken their immortal wages.

I really wanted that poem of Bertie's but by the end of 1962 I
was threatening to do what a more sensible man would have done
long before: to call the whole thing off. Bertie's reply, tactfully
deferred to the day after April Fools' Day, 1963, pleased and
perhaps fooled me. He was writing in bed 'wrapped in a fur of
wheezes'. But 'I'm working away at the Epilogue and am doing
nothing else. Only I'd be grateful if you would give me another
week or so, for it's all in bricks at the moment which have to be
architected.' There had been desperate crises with a landlord and
it was doubtful how long he and his family could stay at Rookery
Farm near Colchester.

I gave him seven weeks. Or, rather, seven weeks passed before I could bring myself to turn from many other pressing things and decide we were no further ahead. I showed both editors a draft letter which I proposed to send to surviving contributors. It was to explain why the project must now be considered to have predeceased them. Louis's answer proposed a conference and magnanimously avoided blame to Bertie. Bertie's reply was written the day after he got my letter and while it was still stinging. '. . . indeed I *have* been working at the Epilogue . . . But I have been frustrated, distracted, tormented and halted by trouble with landlord and solicitors—and the domestic reverberations of it . . . I'll send you this weekend bits of what I've already written, and I'll drive urgently ahead with the whole thing. And I'd be truly grateful if you would hold your hand for the next week or two till I finish it.'

Before the week he sued for was over, he sent me, on 28 May, his finished lines with prose intercalations about how the gaps were to be filled, a sort of preview and 'earnest' of the epilogue, and necessarily a brief one. 'Working on it both excites and depresses me, and I realize that to write about it is like opening an old wound, which is Ireland. However, it is no doubt good for me to do it, and to get rid—in a governed way—of deeply ungoverned bitterness and admiration. I sit here with a little hill before me, of notes, comments, reminiscences, confessions, phrases, lines of verse, thoughts, unthought of, all gathered over mountainous years of trouble and love, and I wonder which way the water—the poetry—which shows the shape of the land, is going to run down it. Will it run, and will the stones obligingly melt? And what dark cloud might pour, on second thought? I have too much, in the past, waited for poetry to run, as one waits for a gift, but gifts get fewer as one waits knowingly for them to come. As Dylan said to me once, "a man's will must be stronger than his gifts". One must prime the pump. I have "will" and wilfulness enough, God knows, to rebuild the hill (apart from depressions) but will it flow? Anyhow, here is the first run ("the first run", they say of Irish whiskey, is fatal; it has to be distilled again and again) for what it's worth. I have to go to Dublin at the end

of June, for a Fred Higgins programme, and this epilogue—or I—
must be finished before that, and in your hands. It'll take me all
my time, resenting myself as I do. But I wish I could get the first
wilful run of it, and then find the easy will-less expansion
of it.'

To me this first run, these fragments shored up against what I
still hoped would not be a ruin, were fine and promised a great
poem; and also to the colleagues to whom, lest I be besotted, I
showed it for confirmation and reassurance. There was nothing
for it but to applaud, and to turn to other work in order to forget
one's impatience.

But fourteen years had passed and we were now in that time
when we must take life not as it comes but as it goes. On the
morning of 30 August that year a friend and I tracked Louis down
to St. Leonard's Hospital where he had been brought in sudden
illness, Louis whom we had all taken for granted as an iron man.
An oxygen cylinder leaned its menacing aid against the wall. His
face was pewter. His eyes, lack-lustre, smiled for us but looked
far beyond us. His voice was weak, his breath short. To try and
cheer him, I told him of a plan to re-issue a book of his. The faint
smile was courtesy to my intention, rather than a poet's pleasure.
We withdrew after a few minutes, shattered. I had seen men, their
bullets fatal, with that colouring, that look. He died early on 3
September.

At the funeral service in St. John's Wood Church, Louis's
world of friends, a bigger world and more various than any of us
would have guessed, came together, some of them apart. In the
pub afterwards, Louis unheard now and unseen still with us, we
held a hurried wake. Bertie told me that from this time forward
the Epilogue, an epilogue to Louis, must be prior to everything,
the finished book would be a memorial.

In October I was myself in Dublin, where Louis was still
mourned. It might be true, the saying Bertie had once repeated
to me, a saying of Cruise O'Brien's father, that Dublin was a holy
city where 'a citizen might see a sparrow fall to the ground every
day and God watching it'.

If God was not watching Bertie's own landfall there in July

1964, Bertie was no doubt keeping a corner of his eye on God; perhaps even deputizing a little, to judge by the Old Testament echo of what he wrote to me from there: 'Probably my reason in going was to vivify my anger and love for the place and to find out why it was always so destructive to the likes of Louis and me. I think that I have found out part of the reason, and I want in some way to get it into the Epilogue of the book. If you can bear with me just a bit longer—I think you said September some time ago— I'll send you a screed. It wasn't an easy visit. I had an AE programme and a 1916 Easter Rising one to deal with, and every day for five weeks I'd to turn myself into a successful extrovert. I think I managed to do it, more equably than usual. But in the small hours of each morning my introverted mind, outraged, had to go mad. AE—Yeats—Dev—Cosgrave, etc., all the old-timers—and all the Words I'd heard about them, would go berserk, become alive, and rampage through my brain with a will of their own but I managed to keep a hold, and to return to civilization.'

That November Laurence Gilliam died, that patron and shield of poets, closing for ever his own old wound, opening one again for others. My own work meanwhile at the office had become ever more demanding and complex, it was more than ever difficult to salvage the energy to write my own stuff, and the thought of Bertie and his epilogue recurred to me only when I was too tired to prevent it and too pessimistic to pursue it. If I was blocked by lack of time to write, Bertie, it now seemed to me, was a hopeless case of writer's block from less external causes. To write the Epilogue he needed to be, not merely the poet he was, but his own confessor, his own priest, his own psycho-analyst. I now doubt whether he was any longer able to make the necessarily appalling self-confrontation. But, then, I rather agreed with him that material uncertainty, the quotidian anxieties of for ever having to find money by ephemeral preoccupations which could not guarantee tomorrow, were the cause. I listened with sympathy to his despair of the hand-to-microphone life, and hoped that he might somehow escape, if only by his own formula, 'Necessity is the mother of circumvention.'

So, like so many of his ancestors and mine, he decided he would cross the Atlantic, go West. I tried to help him to some poetic residency on an American campus. And in February 1966 he wrote to thank me. 'I have not ignored or neglected the "Epilogue". I'm writing some good stuff for it, only it takes a lot of architecting. Also I have to go off on tangents, like organizing Arts Council grants and jobs for young writers in N. Ireland; lecturing, to keep the wolf from the door "in case", as Myles naGopaleen puts it, "he should get out"; finishing a most crying out BBC script for *The Easter Rising*. I'm also despite it all, keeping at the Epilogue, and I think I'm getting my voice back. An accidental, but exacting, bother is that once I get into the Epilogue it starts other hares in my mind and I tend to fly off in pursuit of them and have to remind myself that I haven't the time and that they'll run another day. Like this poem to childhood (I must have started a dozen or two scattered stanzas of it) of which these random stanzas are a sample:

> When I was young
> The day was forever and ever,
> And the bed said
> "Amen".

> The doorknob then
> Was big and sticky with jam, and my
> Forefinger said
> "I am" . . .

'It could go on forever in a half-autobiographical way, half melancholy, half gay, but mounting lyrically (like "Bliss was it in that morn to be alive, And to be young was very Heaven") to some demotic sort of climax like this:

> Hope rose like a bird,
> Fear fell like its turd,
> And all the waters were swinging
> And all the kings were in tatters
> When I was young.

'Maybe I could incorporate it—a poem within a poem—in the Epilogue. But you see what I'm up against. As George Moore said, "If you've been born a dactyl it's difficult to lead a spondaic life". (George was never very good at metre, and Yeats must have been thinking of this on the occasion when he met O'Connor in the Dublin street. "How are you, Yeats?" inquired O'Connor. "Not very well, not very well," said Yeats, "I can only write prose today.")

'Forgive this final delay: it'll be as brief, I promise you, as I can possibly make it, for I'm intent on meeting you and can't meet you without bringing something worth-while in my hand.'

If we met again that year, he brought nothing in his hand. Had he done so, I doubt if the verses, which sound impromptu in his letter, would have survived his sterner judgement. By August he was off to Pitzer College in Claremont, California, the last rainbow with the pot of gold, iron pyrites for a poet. I left him the winter to settle and then reminded him of Louis's memory, a still potent spell. On 6 February 1967, he wrote, sanguine again. He would send the Epilogue in a week. 'I feel like a robin that has got mixed up in a badminton match.' He complained of popularity—his classes were too well attended by the young, which I could well believe. 'To live and move and have your Boeing here, you would need (as an old Austrian friend used to say, referring to the Viennese women) a diesel in your bum, or at least in your elbow.' But he now had a secretary and he was going to write each month or fortnight about articles being revised for the book or replaced. 'For the first time in fifteen years I have steady and stated money coming in to me each month; I can hardly believe it, but it does mean I can plan ahead instead of being at the mercy of misfortune and of myself.

'I hope what I've said will prove to be acceptable in the event. It can't make things worse and it may make them less bitter.'

He was back for that summer in Colchester. Before he went to America he had written to John Hewitt: 'Louis, Spencer, Roethke, Burns-Singer, Brendan—most of them falling off the wires suddenly like October swallows who have been picked off by a delinquent teenage lad with a new air-gun.' Now his own turn

was coming. In Colchester he fell ill and had two serious opera-
tions. I was desk-bound and sessile and did not see him until 20
December in London, the day before he was due to return to
California.

We found him, my wife and I, nominally in bed, at the English-
Speaking Union Club. He was spirited and cheerful, though a
little frail. There was whisky which we drank with water from
the washbasin. He sat up against his pillows and talked a little of
'The Character of Ireland' and much of Ireland's characters. Old
friends like Reggie Smith and Eric Ewens began to appear. It was
not a saloon bar, but at least a saloon bed. For some reason we had
to be back in Oxford by earlyish train. We left him, smiling
among friends. The thought suggested itself that we might not
see him again. I did not accept it. So many had died now, but I
was still not quite out of the stage where one expected everyone
to turn up again.

He went off to California next day, intending to return, but
never to return. There were one or two letters after that, and then
his last letter to me, written on 14 January 1969. 'I thought—and
the doctor thought—that I had emerged successfully from the
wood, but apparently not; two or three trees have been pacing
me.' He was to have another operation next day, in Los Angeles
Hospital. The letter went on to discuss the last stages of 'The
Character of Ireland'. On 2 February we heard on the BBC
night news that he was dead. In the words of John Hewitt's
moving obituary sonnet, 'Now that wild creature is run down
at last.'

Writing of an earlier and less Irish Parnell than ours, Oliver
Goldsmith said: 'A poet, while living, is seldom an object sufficiently great to attract much attention ... When his fame is increased
by time, it is then too late to investigate the peculiarities of his dis-
position; the dews of the morning are past, and we vainly try to
continue the chase by the meridian splendour.' I did not know
Rodgers in the dews of his morning and he had all too little of
time and fame for meridian splendour. Nor is this the place to try
and follow the hare who runs through his poems and his prose as
he ran through life, the hare hounded not only, like Francis

Thompson, by heaven, but by the man himself, the hound in him
and the good in him; that hare that hid in his 'Harvest Field':

> Listen! Listen! do you hear the hiss
> Of the scythe in the long grasses of your laughter?
> More is mowed than you know, for this
> Is Time's swathe, and you are the one that he's after.

But, reading again that desperate renewal of promises, the refrain
of his later letters to me, I see that the problem of the Epilogue was
central to himself. It was to have been his Summa. Into it were to
have gone, all reconciled, the discrete percepts of that mosaic
mind. The expatriate was to have come home; he was to have
been able 'To make the past happen properly, as we want it to
happen': the cat of thought and the mouse of guilt which his
poem, 'The Trinity', could not reconcile were to have settled at
last together in the self to which they are domestic. He had feared
'The shadow of Doubt, that pickpocket of conviction', yet had
hoped, as his Magi on their journey hoped:

> There was nowhere they would not go, feast or fast,
> Slum or salon, bethel or brothel, if only at last
> And at least they could come to the truth and be blessed.

In that Epilogue, there would no longer have been any paradox
in a Presbyterian parson's Europa and the Bull, Pan and Syrinx,
Apollo and Daphne. The Greek, the Roman, and the Orange,
would have been harmonized in an art free as the ancients conceived it and able to comprehend Belfast and Dublin, Wapping,
Colchester and California. Mary Magdalen would have been the
Virgin and there would have been an Ireland such as Wolfe Tone
had imagined, where North and South could be one, when Catholics digging with the left foot and Protestants with the right
would no longer dig one another's graves except in friendship,
and where a new past could be created with room for priest and
presbyter written large or small, a past with room in the same
Irish mind for Carson and for Michael Collins.

Such a poem could not be written in this world, not even in the last refuge of California. The soil could not be removed from the soul till the soul was in the soil, and the bull-man could become a god only when the clod had closed over him. So now the Epilogue, like Robert Emmett's epitaph, cannot be written. Its imago lives only in the Utopia of his poem 'Neither Here nor There', shimmering and beckoning, glimpsed in 'A spool of birds spinning on a shaft of air', whenever the sun burns 'through the meshes of rain'. It is echoed in 'the suck and slap of a spade in the wet clay', and keeps its past promise in our memory of that man of 'undertones, and hesitance, and haze' who has hidden at last in 'the safest place—the bosom of the enemy'.

In a Green Grave

Louis MacNeice

3
In a Green Grave

LOUIS MacNIECE
(1907-1963)

THE fate of some, especially if young, provincial, and eager, is always to arrive too late. The mode has changed, the stars are in a different house, laughter is in another room. The Nazis have changed Berlin; in Italy the trains are on time, those with dangerous thoughts are doing time. The absinthe drinkers have left Paris to the tourists and Pernod; the cubists are merely point three repeating; dada has gone gaga; the vortex has died down, leaving a huguenot and anguished nausea. The Depression has cured the hangovers. In London, the berries of Gordon Square are brown, and only a snicker of Strachey echoes, lingering like a Cheshire sneer. There is no more early Huxley, no more early Waugh. Poetry is punctured by pylons, and pronounced about from Cambridge pulpits. The seventeenth century has returned, by courtesy of Vico, Marx, and Freud; and in the civil war of letters the roundheads of the left are riding down the aesthetes with their long, essenced hair. It is closing time in the gardens of the west.

Or so it seemed to me, arriving too late in Balliol, three years before the war, those same dun, oxen years which MacNeice corralled within the months of his *Autumn Journal*. In Oxford, as elsewhere, the poetry and the fantasy were in retreat before politics; unless, at twenty-three, I was too old and too young to find

45

them, too much an outsider. The earnestness, left and right, of political Balliol might not be surprising, though that Edward Heath should lead those few of its many conservatives who knew they were conservative was a special sign. But where were the poets? Balliol had none. At Merton which had step-mothered Eliot and forborne with MacNeice there was only Blunden. Mac-Neice was the one poet of more or less my own generation for whom I much cared. His feeling felt real. Curb and snaffle he had, but there was a real horse under him. For me the others, hiero-phants of a revolution that smelt of wax candles, anglican, the sweat of highbrows, were future conformists creating an alibi, an elsewhere they could some day cite as an authority for disillusion, psychopomps of the *déja vu* in the passage rites of the *passé*.

Even so, they too had gone their ways and were now bell-wethers in London, town-criers of all power to their elbows and the People. Only choirboys sang now in the roof-trees where Auden and Day-Lewis and Spender had lately, wise thrushlings, sung their songs twice over. MacNeice had gone, too, though in another direction and under other directions. There was a steel rain in Spain and the weather was certain to spread. When *Autumn Journal* appeared, in 1939, the impending *Untergang* was not Stop Press, and I was filling my mind's valise, soon to become a military one, for a short journey to a grave in France.

The journey, as it turned out, was not short or to France but to Greece and Crete and Alamein and Italy and other assignations; though not, the bullets finding an outer and not a bull, with death. When I returned, six years after, many of my friends were dead, and it was late in the day to be making new ones. I had decided that to live was to write, but that to earn a living by writing was not to write well. A double life was to be a solution; poacher by night and gamekeeper by day, I became a publisher.

In the profession of midwife it is as well to like parents as much as babies. And I liked the scholars who wrote the books we pub-lished. But, exotics though they often were, they were not pri-marily writers. They wrote to expound, to elucidate. Their muses were their servants, not their mistresses. They were not writer's writers. The poacher hankered after the company of his kind, the pursuit in midnight coverts of meaning that had to be stalked, netted for, ferreted for, a quarry not known till it was brought down.

So I was often in nocturnal London, where all the game was funeral game. In between the hunt for words and themes, I talked in pubs with others of the trade, in the Lamb, the Wheatsheaf, the Bricklayer's Arms, the Black Horse and, when the fees and writers migrated to the BBC, in the Stag's Head, the Dover Castle, and the George. It was in the Stag, late in 1948, that Jack Dillon—in due time to become the Devlin of *Autumn Sequel*— introduced me to MacNeice.

There was no instant exchange of liking, no immediate synapsis. He was wary of new men. I was a stranger, an ex-soldier marked by a different background and enveloped by a nimbus of different memories. I was an antipodean, a topsy-turvy man; an Irishman who was not of Ireland; an apostate, but from a faith that was not the faith of MacNeice's recent fathers—to use Bertie Rodgers's distinction, a Catholic agnostic, not a Protestant agnostic. I was also a publisher and therefore suspect, though a possible prospect, someone to be treated gingerly.

To me he seemed remote, with an emanation of disdain. He was secure in his own bar and among his own friends, requiring proof that someone he didn't know already was worth knowing, all but supercilious. The guarded eyes machicolated above the cheekbones looked down a long nose. The wry mouth, with its portcullis of long teeth and burglar's underlip, seemed to give a rictus rather than smile, and the laugh sounded like a civil sneer.

We met again, often enough, over the next few months, because we had friends in common. But when we talked it was, as it were, through interpreters, distanced by formal courtesy and protocol. Meanwhile, in 1949, I had been to Dublin. I had gone there with an idea in mind for a collection of articles on Ireland, a book that would transcend the fission of its subject, and display the real order which kept the dance of electrons contained. My visit confirmed that the book would be worth doing. MacNeice and Bertie Rodgers seemed the obvious editors. Both men of Ulster, it was true. But MacNeice's family was from Connemara and he had a Connaught peasant's face, a face I had often seen look up from the spade in Southland's transplanted Galway; and his name was old Irish, a name that went back to Conchubor and Deirdre and Naisi. In his envy of men of action and of the intransigence of his own countrymen he had in mind and understanding, if not in sympathy, the uncompromising obstinacy of the I.R.A. gunman as well as that of the Orange Order. Among his friends were dyed-in-the-wool wearers of the sash their fathers wore, as well as old republican fighters like Peadar O'Donnell. He had called Maud Gonne a 'jumble of opposites' but he too held within himself, though buttoned, those fell opposed points. The name of Ireland, the whole of Ireland, rang in his ears 'Like a bell in an under water belfry'; but, 'educated and domiciled in England', and ruefully glad of it, he knew the sound of the bell was muted. And its music, though disjunctive undersea, was a music to which both sides might listen.

Bertie, too, was an Ulsterman: but one who was later to place proleptically a bunch of beget-me-nots on the empty grave of Paisley and to write:

> . . . I like his people and I like his guts
> But I dislike his gods who always end
> In gun-play.

They both had the freedom of Dublin as well as of Belfast and were trusted in these places where trust was not lightly given. Neutrality alone would not have been enough—only pigs could be in the middle—but love was recognized, like poetry. These were their passports, north and south. Their visas were their verses.

In the middle of June that year they were to come to Oxford to discuss my tentative proposals. The afternoon passed and there was no sign of them, a portent that was not for years yet to be brought home to me, any more than the significance of that day's later sequel. About nine o'clock Bertie rang. Would I join them in the George bar? I flushed them under the window, on the red upholstery, the two of them, and Dylan Thomas. They had come from the other George in London, had drunk but not eaten in the train, and had had a few more jars in Oxford before Bertie nerved himself to ring. They were all three very tight: Dylan boisterous, Bertie portentously grave, and Louis's usual vigilant taciturnity betrayed by the fixture of his smile.

Bertie's awareness of others was a mobile force: it made advances to skirmish or reconnoitre, though it could sometimes ambush. And he had a strong sense of social punctilio, much as a frequent duellist must know the rules, or an old army lag Queen's Regs. He sensed that I wasn't angry at the broken appointment, but none the less felt that protocol required apologies and there would be subtraction from my role and dignity if they were not forthcoming. So, with charm, he solicited a forgiveness already given, and known by him to be given.

Louis was not less aware of others than Bertie. But he looked down and out from the crenellations of his dark tower, noted that I was uneasy, probably guessed that it came from the imbalance of our alcohol, and allowed me to infer all this not from any proffered explanation but by calling to the barman to bring me a pint, watching my progress with it, and quickly ordering up another.

How I might feel was indifferent to Dylan, more exhilarated than the other two, as was his nature. He knew that he could quickly merlinize me. I was simply an interruption to be accorded a minimum and perfunctory pause, or to be exploited for timing and audience. We began talking of Hemingway, how the great marlin of his vanity had played him at the end of his own rod, until he became the original American Old Man of the Me, and brought himself to believe that he was the gamest fisherman in all the sea of letters, and the biggest fish in that sea.

The sign of the fish led to Christianity, and Dylan launched on a parody of a story about the Crucifixion, Hemingway its close-lipped Christ. Delighted with his own virtuosity and our delight he then extemporized a Crucifixion poem by Eliot, *questo il miglior padre*, Golgothic and Gongorian. A parody of Auden came next, and Christ was a young man, an ephebe brainchild of God clinically bleeding, passionately anaemic, a Malcolm Muggeridge made man. Day-Lewis was nailed next, a civilized saviour, and then came Spender, beaming redemption with upturned eyes and down-beat verse, the feet very long.

I listened and laughed, and waited for what I felt Dylan would not be able to resist. He wasn't, and now it was a baroque Irish Bertie who agonized on a cross of tanglewood puns which had somehow become a pulpit as well as a poem. Louis laughed from Parnassus at Bertie so accurately pierced and spreadeagled on his Calvary. Bertie brooded into his pint, amused and mortified, and waiting. And now it was Louis's turn, Apollonian. The water that the Roman spear released from his side was a bloody flux of all the world, and all things flowed, in that sinuous smoke-wreathed *terza rima*, where metaphor slides into metaphor, determining meaning, carrying it like flotsam. Christ became a phoenix burning on Heraclitean fire, and then a Tophet, a top hat of fire, out of which Dylan juggled the rabbits of the one and the many.

When he had finished, it was Bertie's turn to laugh, and I laughed too, Barabbas the publisher. Louis looked down his long nose in rueful acknowledgement of the Welsh wizard and grinned at the three of us.

By now time was called on Calvary, and the torches were put out. We took a taxi to my place, carrying bottles. My wife, adept in men and poets, had the table set and a chicken cooked. There was wine, and coffee afterwards, and more to drink. A couple of bottles later, Dylan had gone uncharacteristically to bed; but Louis and Bertie wanted to see Oxford in the dawn and Louis was convinced it would be a splendid time to discuss with Ernest Stahl, Aloys of *Autumn Sequel*, certain points in the Second Part of Goethe's *Faust*, which Louis was translating for the BBC.

Next day they did not feel disposed, when they surfaced, for talk about our book, and besides there were programmes in London.

> And so to London and down the ever-moving
>   Stairs
> Where a warm wind blows the bodies of men together
>   And blows apart their complexes and cares.

In that London we had many other meetings. But there persisted between Louis and myself that sense of distance, a distance rather than a hostility, a feeling of a tower guarded, sentries not dismissed, a truce not trusted. You could say, I suppose, that among groups of people, or at parties, Louis was not wholly there. He had a presence rather than was present. He was not a dominant, but you knew he was there at the very moment you were feeling he was not. There were times when he seemed to be a dream walking, though he was never the dream of that song. Or perhaps his was the concentration not of the sleep-walker but of the funambulist. You do not interrupt such a walker in the middle of his rope. He is entitled, intent over his Niagara, to the *pas seul* of his narrow, perilous freedom.

And he himself realized that there was always an intention beyond his attention, that his closeness exceeded the merely social.

> So those who carry this birthright and this burden
> Regardless of all else must always listen
> On the odd chance some fact or freak or phantom
> Might tell them what they want, might burst the cordon
> Which isolates them from their inmost vision.

Late in 1949 he went to Athens as Director of the British Institute and I did not see him till the March of 1952 when he and Bertie came again to Oxford, this time uncompanioned by Silenus, and sober. We reached what seemed to be a firm plan for the book, and I was off to New York the following day.

It changed again and again, as the years passed, this plan of ours. Defaulters came and went, and from the margins new ideas infiltrated into the room of the old. It was a palimpsest, the draft of a dual poem—so much of whose verse stayed blank—and the two poets were merciless in their meddling and muddling towards perfection. But even at an early stage I began to worry that nothing would ever be finished unless a stability of intention were imposed. In October that year I asked for a consultation which I was determined would be a confrontation.

We met at Oddenino's, still a place then, but now only a diminishing echo, a name written in remembered wine. It was a burgundy we drank as we ate and there was a great deal done of both. At coffee I made an attempt to pin down my dragonflies.

They easily eluded me, taking off into shimmering flights of words. If we decided anything I do not remember. The only note I could afterwards decipher suggests that nothing was said, in a business sense, to be worth remembering. The egos of poets, like the livers of Strasbourg geese, are specialized and overfeeding produces poetry or *pâté*. It is my memory's weak custody of the poetry that I regret.

When the waiters closed in on us, the pubs outside were closed, and we were dry from drinking. But Bertie knew an Italian club in Soho. We had become grave and responsible men of business, practical men. It was obviously necessary that we should continue our still inchoate discussion over a drink. We would have only a jar or two and go our ways. For I was to be taken that night by a friend to Gielgud's *Much Ado;* a friend of Bertie's had tickets for *Porgy and Bess;* and Louis and Hedli were to go to a film of Everest whether because it was there or because he had written the script. We nodded at one another, with sage approval of our sobriety and restraint, getting our satisfaction from these virtues in advance of displaying them.

In those days I had a hard head and a good liver, which is perhaps why I have neither now. But the copious Chianti eventually got to me and released the black Irish anger normally contained. For the hundredth time, it suddenly seemed, Bertie was explaining Ireland to me. I was being treated like a publisher and a sassenach. Was I not myself a poet and an Irishman? I rebelled, a genetic and national inveteracy. I had a better claim to speak, I taunted. He was only presbyterian plantation Irish, little better than a Scotsman, and a lowlander at that. Bertie's brown eyes enlarged with offence and anger. But, non-practising parson though he was, he was no Paisley but a man of peace. He got up in prudent dudgeon and departed.

Louis, always a *tête dure*, was laughing through the smoke of his Sweet Afton cigarette. But when a third leaves in anger it is wise for the remaining two to go elsewhere. Besides, the pubs were now open. We went to the nearby Mooney's and drank draught Guinness, talking of one of Louis's passionate preoccupations, Rugby football. But I had a preoccupation of my own. My little luxury of rage was too rare to be thrown away so soon, even though Bertie's going had given it a temporary check. The bottle was still half full, the cork in the fireplace.

I remembered the story of the set-to between Louis and the swashbuckling Roy Campbell. Louis had reproached Campbell in some pub or other for having struck a poet, a man weaker than himself. 'It was only a bit of a pat, like this', Campbell had replied, tapping Louis lightly. 'I don't believe you', Louis said. 'I think it was a real swipe, like this.' And he had slapped Campbell's face, hard.

Louis, then, was a man of his hands, more suitable for abuse than Bertie, no fighter with his fists. He was the target I needed. He too was a black Ulster Protestant, I told him. And what was there to choose between a black Presbyterian and a black Anglican? Weren't they both orange? Wasn't his father a bishop, with a diocese of acres but not of souls? Wasn't he himself 'banned for ever from the candles of the Irish poor'? But Louis, remembering perhaps how his father had refused to sign the 1912 Covenant, only gave his lopsided smile. I could not get behind the guard of his good humour. And, as I gave up groping for shrewder insults, time—not the publican's time for once—suddenly arrested us, and we remembered we had our theatres to go to. My anger had burnt out, Louis was affable to the embarrassment in my apologies, and we went our ways.

I did not get to my theatre. Bertie was ordered to bed when he got home and snored while Porgy sang to Bess. Only Louis, tenacious of purpose, got as far as Everest, though he slept before the peak.

It was a year before we met again. Louis had come to Oxford on that visit commemorated in *Autumn Sequel*, where 'the years like small dun oxen crash the ford.' It was October, when Oxford 'seems all dead stone (which here hath many a Fellow).' The visit was dedicated to the piety of other and older friendships—Professor Dodds (Boyce of the poem) and Ernest Stahl being principal, 'two soft-spoken men in a firelit room'. For, slow to make friends, Louis was even slower to relinquish friendship, and neither time nor distance ever weakened the affections he so discriminatingly

gave. And now, as on all his other visits to Oxford, there were
memories of himself when young and in love:

> I pass the shop where Esther, a slim girl,
> Chose herself roses for a ball. . . .

Our own encounter lasted longer than the phrase he gives it—
'the foregone conclusion of a business lunch.' At the table in the
Randolph he talked, the business concluded and in part foregone,
of Mariette his first wife, the slim girl who chose roses, roses all
the way. It had been with her mother that he was first infatuated,
sitting at her feet in a house that recalled Troy and Byzantium and
Istanbul, Athens and Chios and Crete, all the Aegeans from
Homer to Seferis. Then one night Mariette had descended the
stairs dressed for a ball.

Her mother, the dragon-wife of a great scholar and possessive
in all her attachments, did not relish the transfer. I could see why
it had been so. I had met her myself, twenty years older but in old
age still formidable, not a queen who would have yielded con-
quest lightly. By then her will to dominate had become a will to
use, for her husband's sake, she the guardian priestess of his time
and learning.

Talking of them, we walked along St. Giles' and Louis pointed
out the house where that stair still turned, though the vision had
fled. No *figlia che piange* but a girl who had left him and for whom
he had wept. It was the first time he had spoken to me of the self
he had been, the self that he still most truly and deeply was. For
no man was more tenacious of his past. I felt for the first time that
we were friends, and that it would remain so.

Afterwards, I wondered to Bertie about this change. It was
because you got drunk together, he said, that day of the lunch in
London. Louis never trusts anyone until they have been drunk
with him. After that, if he still likes them, he doesn't change. In
friendship he is like a virgin, recalcitrant. Friendship means so
much to him that at first he kicks against the pricks.

Other things were changing. Bertie and Marianne Gilliam were
to marry, and we all met in the White Room in London to cele-

brate, and dined afterwards in the Café Royal. Not long afterwards Dylan Thomas died. No one grieved more than Louis and
there is no more splendid memorial to Dylan than the laughing,
buoyant poet forever resurgent in *Autumn Sequel*:

> . . . young and gay,
> A bulbous Taliessin, a spruce and small
>
> Bow-tied Silenus roistering his way
> Through lands of fruit and fable, well aware
> That even Dionysus has his day.

And it is true that Louis was a great cherisher of friendships,
polishing them and fingering them in his memory like beads,
intoning their names in *Autumn Sequel* like a litany.

Nowadays whenever he was in Oxford he included us in his
round of pieties and usually stayed the night. He and I had both
read Greats, and with me he could speak in the shorthand of
classical allusion. For the man who has read Latin and Greek in
our time is like the bearer of a secret prohibited knowledge. He
must reveal it, as the Irish in the days of the Penal Laws spoke
Irish, only among those who also know it. Otherwise, his allu-
sions will not be understood, or will be thought an insolent affecta-
tion. We do not live in the time of the Guardians, not yet, but
Plato is now, nonetheless, a treasonous clerk.

Similarly, he got on well with my wife, partly because her
memory was so well stocked with poetry. Once she reminded
him of the lines in *Autumn Sequel*—'Save me, Lamb and Flag,
Pray for me, Eagle and Child'—and congratulated him on the
chiasmus of the Christian and imperial symbols. 'Chiasmus?' he
said. 'I hadn't noticed it. I was thinking only of the two pubs on
the opposite sides of St. Giles', and how often I had fled to them.'

My wife's circadian rhythms matched better in those days with
late hours than mine and occasionally he would turn up at short
warning and they would sit up long into the night talking. I
remember one night when I had already gone to bed, after vainly
expecting him until the local pub closed. Shortly afterwards,
bringing his hostess for dinner as evidence that he had been un-
avoidably but justifiably delayed, he arrived. I got up again and

we drank a choice of gin or tea. We talked about John Malcolm Brinnin's book on Dylan, and laughed at the review of it that Dylan might be writing somewhere with brimstone on asbestos. Then my wife persuaded Louis to read a poem of his own, something he did rarely, at least with us. It was 'April Fool', which he had lately finished, this being May.

> Here come I, old April Fool,
> Between the hoar frost and the fall.
> Fool me drunk and fool me dry,
> Spring comes back, and back come I.

He was in his fiftieth year then, and the hoar frost was in his hair, and on his mind the rime. He was conscious of that paradox of time that overtakes us, the ageing house, and our recalcitrance that we, the tenants, are still the same old identities, some of them at least still young. And the following September on his birthday, in the ML Club—where, as Ian Rodger said, it is always afternoon —he pointed to the grey hairs, a few of them, in his temple, and gave me his wry smile. I remembered the smile later, reading, 'It came to me on the Nile my passport lied, Calling me dark who am grey.'

Death was no less busy than usual in those years, and we were all by now of an age to be reminded constantly that we were vulnerable; that, though everyone does not live, everybody dies. In 1957 Joyce Cary died, and my wife was much preoccupied with arranging his papers and preparing the final version of his posthumous novel. Once she took Louis to the empty house where the dead man's presence seemed still a living thing. While she worked among the papers Louis fingered the rhyming dictionary that Joyce had put together when he was writing his poems. Louis kept it in his hands, long and marvelling, a man himself obsessed with rhyme, and the ways it opened to one's undiscovered meanings, the discipline and rules it imposed on their expression, as the walls of a squash court impose a certain pattern of behaviour on the ball and players.

Time, too, brought the penalties of a certain fame, more grotesque in our day. For oblivion is no longer permitted, now that literature has become an academic subject, to do its dung-beetle task. Writers have become the honey-cows of academic ants and are milked sedulously of manuscript. Foul papers are the un-skimmed milk and it is the first draft rather than the last which qualifies for the museum's immortality. Almost any scrap of paper is oil to Texas, something to be shuffled off to Buffalo.

For Louis there was something sinister about libraries and museums: however the scholar in him might value them, in his poetry they tend to symbolize *nature morte*, life dead and so sus-ceptible of control, the immortal shrivelled to the immortelle. He went in dread of their touts and scavengers, at that time plentiful in the literary bars and clubs. Once he surprised an ardent middle-man groping in his office wastepaper basket. And in the ML Club when he wanted to read the draft of a new poem he would draw us aside first into a safe corner. 'That man' was over there. Yet one must concede that he himself, in hard times, had had trans-actions with 'that man'. This fact was now a factor in his dislike.

One poem to be jealously concealed was the long-promised Prologue to 'The Character of Ireland'. He had travelled a great deal in the years since the war—in Greece, India, Africa, and South Africa ('What must it be like in a country governed by mad babies?' he said of the latter), in the United States and the Far East. Though his feeling for Ireland was as intense as ever, the poem divulged an impatience with the provincialism of the Irish quarrel:

> To the tourist
> This land may seem a dreamland, an escape,
> But to her sons and even more her daughters
> A dream from which they yearn to wake; the liner
> Outhoots the owls of the past. The saffron kilt
> May vie with the Orange sash but the black and white
> Of the press of the rest of the world scales down their feuds
> To storms in a teacup. What is the Border
> Compared with the mushroom fears of the dizzy globe
> In which no borders hold?

Nevertheless, he resumes:

We who were born in this land of words and water
Know that to judge a love by the facts alone—
And even should the affair be ended—means
To say it never happened. Which is false.
What happened must persist.

And so, he seems to say, the poetry and life of Ireland still flow
on beneath the quotidian and provincial prose, even when we
forget or are too exasperated to see them:

> So the eye
> Can miss the current in a stream, the ear
> Ignore even a waterfall, the mind,
> Intent on solid fact, forget that water,
> Which early thinkers thought the source of all things,
> Remains the symbol of our life; yet never,
> No more than peat can turn again to forest,
> No more than the die, once cast, can change its spots,
> No more than a child can disavow its birthplace,
> No more than one's first love can be forgotten,
> If pressed, could we deny this water flows.

His own stream was passing now through steeper banks. His
marriage had come under a late and breaking strain. He seemed
deeply depressed in himself. He would throw it off when he came
down to stay in Oxford. His visit for the 1961 election to the
Chair of Poetry gave him rich amusement, even if his relish was
somewhat sardonic and he interpreted such remarks as 'the corpses
are nominating the killer' as being deeper than the donnish witti-
cisms they were meant to be. Another time he was preparing a
programme on Oxford stone and we took him to visit quarries in
the Cotswolds, and one could see his mind playing with the various uses of the stone, his imagination not very far from the
mortality that flaking stuff so often covered, the holes it left
behind and the holes it stopped, thoughts of permanence and
passage.

One could see him in these years trying to come to terms with
the Laocoön of middle age, wrestling in unspoken desperateness
with something he knew could not be cured but seemed reluctant

to endure. In the Irish way, and in the way of gregarious writers everywhere, he had always made much use of alcohol and pubs, was at home in them sometimes it seemed more than he was at home. He had never sought an exclusively literary company. For him, a 'maker' could as well be a man of action as a man of letters. He liked men who played games well, men who worked provided that they did work, men who made things with their hands —he once told my wife that if he had a second life to live he would have liked to make things in a medium other than words, to carve in wood perhaps or in stone. He liked men of strength and courage, hard men.

But often in these later years the hard men were the hard drinkers. He seemed to need the company of men who could keep it up all night, and not for just one night. I remember a chance meeting with him one morning in the York Minster before it became too genteel to serve pints. Of the two men with him, one was barely awake and the other could scarcely overcome an aphasia. Louis's own voice was reduced to a raucous croak, his eyelids were canopies, and the set of his mouth was diagonal. I gathered they had not been in bed for two nights running. Louis indeed made me think of a sleep-walking pedestrian who has wakened in the middle of a zebra crossing and sees that there is no further side. He seemed to be on the run from himself, from some kind of despair.

> The dove's is now the raven's day
> And there is interest yet to pay;
> And in those branches, gibbet-bare,
> Is that a noose that dangles there?

Those lines from *Visitations* were written a few years before this time but the mood they suggest seemed now to have become almost dominant. He may have been at some crisis of his creative powers, the springs blocked, the images within fixed in some intolerable pattern. If so, he was using alcohol to jolt the frozen kaleidoscope, was kicking against his life as one kicks an obdurate machine. Or he may have hoped that by resuming some earlier pattern of wildness he could recapture the youth and excitement, the escape, that a prolonged pub-crawl can sometimes manage when one is in one's twenties but which eludes one later, when it has a sinister resemblance to self-destruction and the magic mist which sheltered the epic hero becomes merely a cloud of voluntary unknowing, a shroud to the consciousness.

He came out of this in a year or so, in a way that we did not expect, through a new and sudden love affair. Such things have the advantage that they confer afresh from outside an endorsement of a man's failing regard for himself. In the lyrical release, the reopening of emotion and wonder, his own lyrical gift was freed again. The siege of the dark tower was lifted. It must have been about this time that he began to write the poems of his last book, *The Burning Perch*. Though he seemed serene in the few years that followed, and claimed to be happy, there is a grimness under the surface. A second spring must always be less innocent than the first, because it remembers the winters that lie between, and the last winter to follow. 'They were introduced in a grave glade,' runs the first line of one poem; and it ends with the line, 'They were introduced in a green grave.'

There seemed to be gaiety and life dancing over that green glade, however, and towards the end of 1963 I made yet another effort to bring our book to the printer's bed. On 29 August I came to the George in search of Louis, at the end of a day in London. He had been ill, people said, and hadn't been round lately. Someone reported that his sister had gone to see him in Tring where he was living, had found him up and about but obviously ill, and had taken him to St. Leonard's Hospital. He had been doing a programme near Porlock about potholing, and his conscientious craftsmanship—or perhaps an Orpheus-like preoccupation with the underground and the abodes of Dis which recurs from time to time in his life and in his verse—made him feel he had to go underground himself. He had caught a chill, neglected it, and there was talk of pneumonia.

I decided to stay the night in London and try to see him next morning. I had always thought of him physically as an iron man; and the idea of his being ill struck me as wrong, out of place, menacing. With another friend, Martha McCulloch, I went to see him next day. He was very ill, very cold, his face the colour of an Irish winter sea and sky. I did not like to worry him about our book but told him, to please him, that my colleagues wanted to reprint his early study of Yeats. His smile glimmered, but only to please me. He was himself beyond pleasure. I dropped the idea of asking him to write a new preface. For this was not the face of a man who would breathe much longer, and I felt in my bones that he would not live to write again.

He asked for a novel of Iris Murdoch's when we offered to get him anything he wanted. Not to tire him, we came away. We looked at each other outside, each hoping not to find in the other's eyes the confirmation of what each thought. 'Poor Louis is for the high jump, I'm afraid,' I said, falling back on the phrase we had used in the war when death had more often to be mocked. She nodded, unable to speak.

I had to go back to Oxford, after the foregone conclusion of another business lunch. On the way to Paddington I remembered all those times at the George, the efforts to break away from the excitement of friends, and Louis, the centre of a little world of poets, a world that would die with him, and then the anxious pursuit of taxis, and the nearly missed trains, with the laughter and the stories still echoing in one's mind. In the train, this last time, I kept seeing that mortal face, the sentry in the dark tower confronting now his final enemy. I had left London for Oxford so often, leaving life behind me. One life now would never follow.

Louis's sister Elizabeth and his second Mary stayed with him day and night from then on at the hospital. Early on the Tuesday morning Elizabeth telephoned Martha McCulloch to bring a transistor radio. Louis wanted music. She brought one to the hospital in the late morning. But the string quartet that had been all tuned up in the back of his mind when he wrote of the meeting in the grave glade had now found somewhere to go. The strings, true or false, would no longer vibrate in that memory. He had returned to his own full past, that past which like all our pasts had seemed never so full that it could not take another draught of time and living and love. More power, power to the Makers. Of whom, he made as well as any.

The Chinese Box

Enid Starkie

Portrait by Patrick George

4

The Chinese Box

ENID STARKIE
(1897–1970)

IN Oxford after the war, Walton Street, Little Clarendon Street,
and St. Giles' became my daily dog-legged axis. The same
streets were regularly traversed by a vivid small woman who
always wore either a red jacket and blue trousers or a blue jacket
and red trousers. In those days few women wore trousers and to
wear them implied an assertion. Even without this, one would
have guessed from the firm straight nose, the intensely blue eyes,
and the defiantly dyed red hair curling in mutiny from under a
red or blue beret, that here was an unusual, an independent, spirit.

One day Ronald Syme identified her for me: 'That's Enid
Starkie. Our Enid.' The name was familiar. The Clarendon Press
had published her *Rimbaud in Abyssinia*, though in 1937, before
my time. And her autobiography, *A Lady's Child*, had seemed to
me to have in it something of Katherine Mansfield: they both
came from a family of one son and four daughters, middle class,
each family prominent in a provincial capital. Bourgeois Wellington and bourgeois Dublin had much in common, and there were
likenesses also between Enid Starkie's Cushendun and Katherine's
'At the Bay'.

Ronald Syme made vague promises of introduction which I
did not press. Formal meetings with the famous were apt not to
prosper. Time and chance could no doubt be trusted. A couple of

years later they did indeed co-operate. Keith Scott-Watson, an old friend from wartime Cairo, turned up, a former journalist and fearless of celebrities. He wanted to meet Dr. Starkie and arranged it through a friend of both, Nicholas de Watteville. My wife and I, as Keith's hosts, were asked along as well.

We all met after dinner in White's Bar, then just becoming free of American servicemen. Enid drank Irish and soda, the rest of us beer. Closing time surprised us, still garrulous and thirsty. So, at Enid's suggestion, persuasively hospitable, we went to her flat at 41 St. Giles' and were duly done the honours of that showpiece, at once a shrine of family memories, a treasury that displayed the triumphs of her tenacious taste from many an auction and antique shop, and the carapace which shielded the scholar and the woman. I noted the difference between the upstairs study, comfortable but austere, with its French frieze of paper-bound books, her working library, and the downstairs drawing-room, splendid in red lacquer and gold. In the one she was a worker bee, industrious among the combs; in the other a humming-bird, hovering over each guest in turn, plying us with Irish whiskey.

She was quick and direct and warm. Friendship grew between us and one recognized the feeling as real. She commented on the 'Irishness' of my face, 'I always recognize an Irish face.' She reproved and refuted, though without confuting, a remark of mine that she was 'Anglo-Irish' or 'Ascendancy'. She elicited that we were 'lapsed Catholics' and volunteered that she was a 'bad Catholic'. When I suggested she might yet become a relapsed one, she did not deny that she was keeping her options open.

From then on we met frequently at parties, since I was able to persuade myself that going to them was really my duty as a publisher and she, because she loved social life and was able to communicate enjoyment to everyone around her, was asked to everything. More often than not we found ourselves drawn into the orbit of her vitality, the zest that made her seem our younger contemporary.

In those days we used to meet friends for drinks in some regular pub on Saturday mornings, after visiting the bookshops; a celebration of the fact that the working week was over and a preliminary to retiring for the interval before Monday recurred, an interval when I could work on writing of my own. Enid, too, had long set herself the challenge of leading a full social and teaching life and yet somehow reserving the time—usually stolen from sleep—to do her own work. Pubs were not really her milieu: the lady's child in her still imposed some inhibitions, and as long as we knew her she would never drink in a bar, or even enter it, by herself; if she were the first to arrive she would wander about disconsolately outside, even if it were snowing and there was a warm fire in the bar and she herself well known there. Nevertheless, she easily fell in with our Saturday morning routine, especially as the Lamb and Flag, our local in those days, was just across St. Giles' from her flat.

It was about this time that she brought back from France her Breton sailor's hat with its pompon rouge. 'What's the name of your ship, lady?' a man once accosted her outside the pub. 'I'd like to stow away on her.' It was a good period, even allowing that any period is good once it is long enough over and if you were young in it. People from the whole range of academic disciplines, scientists and arts dons, writer friends from London and further afield, old friends from the war and before the war, Africans and Americans and Japanese and Chinese, stray visitors from anywhere in the world, all gathered in the public bar for an hour or two, lively and still young enough to have time and not be tied to set hours for lunch. If no man could any longer be a Leonardo, I thought, at least you could construct through a group a composite renaissance personality.

Sometimes, though, we preferred a tête-à-tête, and Enid and I would meet in the Eagle and Child before crossing the road to the larger company. With only one for audience she was less assertive and did not talk for victory as she was apt to do when there were many present. Her conversation always tended towards a musical structure: first a statement of theme and then endless variations and repetitions in a pattern so dense and complex that, as with music, you emerged at the end less with a reasoned argument or even conviction than with a cloudy feeling, an impression only, of what the original statement had been. At times, when she was heated by opposition, she would hammer away at her thesis as if it were a Hungarian rhapsody of Liszt's.

In private she was more relaxed, the fingers on the keys gentler and more tender. She talked much of the past, would wonder whether she had done right to abandon a career as a pianist for scholarship. Or scenes familiar to me from *A Lady's Child* would be re-enacted, with fresh detail from her minutely exact memory, or new emphasis. She would recall, with perplexity still resentful and that lively Irish sense of injustice, how Mademoiselle had accused her of always wanting to be different, and of always arguing. '*Elle raisonne toujours.*' Though I did not say so, I knew what Mademoiselle meant. Yet it was true that Enid, or at least one side of her, did really want to be like everyone else and did want to be compliant, reasonable. But a much stronger side of her wanted nothing of the kind, though she would seldom admit to its existence. And the *esprit fort* which her father had discerned and valued in her was as often as not engaged in supporting the character she preferred to see herself as—the sensitive, misunderstood, grown-up child. It was in these conversations that I began to see how much her father still dominated her life and character. The habit of seeking his approbation had made her a pleonect of praise and, though he was dead, she still bent towards him like a sunflower after sunset. He had set her standard, by his example, of what she conceived scholarship should be, and she was unresting in emulation. She had promised in his unconscious ear as he was dying, 'I shall do the things you wanted me to do. I shall try and make a success of an academic career.' It had been a real promise; for to Enid all promises were real, even those one made to oneself.

She talked, too, of Paris, of the hard life she had led there while working for her Sorbonne doctorate, determined to support herself and sometimes having to do the most menial, skivvying jobs to survive. It was in those days that she had had to develop prowess as a *pique-assiette*, a scrounger by necessity, and she recalled her feats in this line with a pride which sublimated the deeper pride her poverty had compelled her to subdue. Presumably Paris had not been only crust and water and rags and work,

but if there had been men in her life in those days—and one sometimes suspected that she had rather a prolonged virginity to con-
ceal—she did not talk of them. One gathered that then or later
she had 'lived' but she was always reticent about the deeper side
of her relations with others, even when I knew her much better;
a reticence to be respected and recognized as not uncommon in
loquacious people. Those who talk much of themselves have to
impose on themselves certain disciplines of reserve, if they are not
to become dispersed totally. I speculated, but to myself, why she
had never married, very attractive as she must have been. That
promise to her father would have been part of it, a dedication that
required control over her own solitudes. And there was also her
fierce sense of self, the 'jealous feeling of sole ownership of myself',
which she first remembered experiencing when someone picked
her up, a baby, and she clung to her own toes, closing the circle
of herself, resentful and powerless in the alien lap.

On a cabinet in her flat there was the photograph of a young
man, a ballet dancer. 'He was a Russian, I forget his name. I knew
him in Paris,' she said demurely. But the solitary photograph, the
beauty of the young man, her eyes when she failed to remember
his name, she who remembered everyone's name, suggested discretion, not amnesia.

By the time we met Enid we already knew Joyce Cary. He and
Enid were friends of long standing. They had first met about the
time his *House of Children* and her *A Lady's Child* were published,
in 1941. Joyce took no interest in reviews of his books and read
only those which his wife thought might be worth his trouble.
For Enid, however, reviews were an essential part of a writer's
life. She extorted from them the last grain of feeling, whether
pleasure or irritation. She always knew what journals had reviewed
a book of hers, what critics. Not that hostility or neglect would
make her change her own estimate of her book's value. It was
simply a matter of vital import to her what others thought of her
work, and therefore of her, as it might be to a girl how many
times she had been asked to dance and by whom, even if she had
no need to count in order to be certain that she was attractive. To
know one's own worth was not enough; it had to be endorsed by

the world. 'I don't know why the reviewers made such a fuss of your book, Joyce,' she would say. 'Of course, it's a very good book but, all the same, it's not as much better than mine as all that. Mine is a very good book too. And they're both autobiographies, really, though I know you'll say yours isn't an autobiography but a novel. And they're both about growing up in Ireland. I suppose it must be that the reviewers have got me typed as a scholar, someone they don't expect to write about herself. Whereas you're a novelist and so it's all right for you. They ought to judge by the book itself, though, not by what they expect.' And Joyce would smile, with one eye screwed up, that merry quizzical fond smile of his.

It was the habit of his friends to drop in at his house in Parks Road of a Sunday evening before dinner. Enid was at her best on these occasions. Joyce would be sitting back in the sofa, twinkling and delighting in her as she stood on the carpet before the fireplace, perilously waving her glass of gin and French—Irish and soda was her pub drink—and too full of energy to sit. She would be on some favourite theme of hers, the superiority of French men over English in their attitude to women, perhaps. Her speech was emphatic, helped out by those gestures which endangered the gin and the carpet, rapid and leaving no opening for interruption, the Irish accent marked but full of Dublin Ascendancy confidence. 'No, Joyce, there's no good denying it, Englishmen just don't like women. They may have to have them, mothers, sisters, daughters, wives, mistresses even, but they don't really like them. You can't say they do, Joyce, not really like them, I mean. Whereas a Frenchman actually prefers, really does prefer, the company of women to that of men. He doesn't shut himself away in pubs or clubs, and look at women as if they were intruders.'

You couldn't wedge a protest into all this without being bounced off by some argument *ad hominem*. If I tried it, for example, she would soon put me down. 'No, Dan, you can't talk, you're not English, you're a New Zealander, and you're Irish anyway, and the Irish are different, more like the French. Besides, you're the sort of man women always spoil, so you're bound to like them anyway.' The bright blue eyes would glint at everyone as she spoke and she would fail to notice the centrifugal swivel she had given her glass. Then she'd be away again. 'Now look at the way a Frenchman looks at a women, he's looking at her as a woman and not just as an inferior sort of man—'

On occasions like this her dress was informal, though of course it was a uniform, that combination of jacket and trousers in blue and red, her assertion that she was an emancipated post-war woman, the peer of men—even if it was not always recognized as such: an American friend of mine, seeing her for the first time, had mistaken her for a bus conductor coming off duty. But she had been brought up, after all, in late-Edwardian Dublin, the formal ambience of which her bohemian clothes marked the repudiation. And the rejection was not complete. There were times, at the big set dinner parties she loved or grand College occasions, when her suppressed Edwardian self would re-emerge. The sort of dress she then delighted to wear would not have been out of place in her mother's drawing-room, something she might have worn when she was sixteen—a pink or a Child-of-Mary blue gown instead of the scarlet and Prussian blue of her daytime self. A round-eyed débutante replaced her unconventional persona and she became a stickler for protocol—she would insist on yielding precedence through a doorway to any married woman present, however much younger than herself. The more courses the dinner had the better it was, especially if things like smoked salmon or caviare were among them. And a dinner wasn't really a dinner unless there were ices. If there were mint sorbet in the middle, that was best of all.

For the wines she was able to switch characters and reserve the right to be as critical as any man—she was, after all, Somerville cellar-keeper, the veteran of years of wine-tasting parties, an honoured guest every year at Dolamore's special party at Lord's. Alas, the effect of the genuine expertise was often marred by the intervention of an even younger self of hers. In *A Lady's Child* she describes how on Sundays the children always came down from the nursery for formal lunch and how invariably 'through some unfortunate misadventure, I always spilt a glass of water'. She had never been able to lose this habit of misadventure, in fact the habit of excited gesture, eyes on her *vis-à-vis*, to emphasize her point. Only now it was claret, not water, that toppled and swiftly spread its tell-tale stain like blood across the table.

Any kind of ceremonial occasion, any ritual, brought out the strain of the child in her. In those days she usually had two Christmas dinners, at midday with one family of friends, at night with another. As the years went by one of the dinners was usually with us. Our children were small then, but even their eyes were not bigger and rounder than Enid's when the goose had been carved, the plum pudding and brandy butter eaten, the crackers exploded and the mottoes read and the paper hats donned, and by candlelight the presents were distributed from under the Christmas tree.

On Boxing Day till Joyce Cary died there was a huge family expedition, organized by Joyce, to the pantomime. Enid would be among the children and the chocolates, impatient for the curtain. I was usually in a subdued state of hangover myself, barely alive to enjoy the legs of the Principal Boy and the chorus; but before my eyes closed in discreet slumber I would see Enid, mouth a little open and blue eyes full of wonder at some good fairy's intervention or, switching selves, full of mirth at some dubious *double entendre* of the funny men And, back at Parks Road for tea, she would be exulting in the family gathering, as full of life and love and warmth as she must have been long ago when a child in Dublin.

But nothing animated her as much as a cause, preferably a forlorn hope, a last-ditch battle. She was not so much interested in politics at large; if she had once been left wing, she was now left bank. Nowadays her battles were local. It might be some struggle in College, or in the Faculty Board, a possible nomination— usually improbable—for the Nobel Prize, a suitable or, better still, unsuitable candidate for an honorary degree. Under pledges of discretion, she would bring out her elaborate dossier of the campaign she had fought single-handed and single-minded against Sir Richard Livingstone, the Vice-Chancellor of the time, to get an honorary degree for André Gide. She was full of scorn for those who might have helped but didn't—afraid, she suggested, that they might have been thought to share his sexual ambiguity. She had less trouble when she took up the struggle to do the same for Jean Cocteau; but by then times and Vice-Chancellors had changed, and others had learned the futility of opposition, even those whom she scathingly denounced as hedgers and ditchers— those who hedged their support with impossible conditions and those who ditched her and her candidate at the last fence.

An election for the Chair of Poetry especially dilated her nostrils. She argued, after Maurice Bowra's term of office, that the Chair ought to go to someone outside the University, to someone who would not otherwise be heard in Oxford. And he should be a practising poet: there were enough people already engaged in talking about poetry as critics, indeed too many. Having decided on her poet—in 1951 Cecil Day-Lewis, in 1956 W. H. Auden— she would then ascertain if he were willing to stand, bullying or cajoling him if necessary. Next she would canvass, by letter or in person, all those entitled to vote and would publish as soon as possible in the *Gazette*, so as to deter rivals, her formidable list of supporters.

The whole campaign would be conducted with a zest and panache that inevitably attracted the interest of the popular Press. Enid herself, partly through craft and partly through innocence, was natural copy. She could never quite grasp that to a popular journalist a story is literally a 'story', that it is not the facts that matter for him but what can be done with them. She could not resist the press photographer's visit, the interrogation by telephone from Fleet Street, however often she ended with the wry realization that 'all they want to know is whether I wear scarlet knickers'. And, anyhow, it was all part of the excitement, the feeling of total commitment to a cause, the heady satisfaction of energies fully engaged, of enemies defeated, of a role and a stage and limelight.

But these were the good years, the 1950s, and she had energy for everything—university politics, the cherishing of her research students, the faithful correspondence with old pupils, a deep and fanatical interest in the affairs of her College and an active sympathy with the young, social life, and the writing of her own books. In the formal capacity of publisher I looked after only her

Zaharoff Lecture, *Arthur Rimbaud 1854–1954*, but she talked much to me as she did to other friends about the rest of her books while she was writing them for other publishers. The books themselves came steadily: *André Gide* in 1953 and *Petrus Borel* in 1954, the new edition of *Baudelaire* in 1957, *Gautier to Eliot* in 1960, the third edition of *Arthur Rimbaud* in 1961.

Her method was to track down and assemble every scrap of material she could find in private collections, newspaper files, or libraries and then, in the light of the author's own works and of the secondary writings, traverse all the material afresh. As she wrote to me when she sent me the typescript of *Baudelaire*—the only copy and I must not only guard it with my life but remember to return the rubber bands round each chapter because they were of a special kind and size and like the typescript itself irreplaceable —'only another biographer would realize out of what tiny scraps the life has been built'. Her strength lay in the diligence with which she hunted down and recognized the significance of these scraps, the perception which she brought to their interpretation, the skill with which she fitted in and reconstructed from the scattered fragments of the jigsaw its original pattern.

In the handling of general ideas she was less at home, though she would not have admitted this. Her weakest book is *Gautier to Eliot*, which sets out to be a discussion of symbolism, but which suffers not only from an insecure grounding on the English side of the subject but also from a certain failing at the conceptual, plastic level, the level of abstract argument. She needed to be close to a personality for her passion to be really roused. It was where her piety to the facts could be put at the service of her human sympathy that she wrote best. And this is already much: facts, once established, are firm, but conceptual flights and psychological and aesthetic theories are kites which have to come down, fashions which change with each generation.

Her style at its best was plain, as was fitting for her aims and her matter. In her later work it suffered somewhat from the habits of the lecturer—what I tell you three times is true and you are more likely to remember what I say if I repeat it. And there were too many signs of weariness and the resolution to finish in spite of odds. Reading her *Baudelaire* typescript for her by way of friend-ship I felt I could almost determine by the number of typing slips, by the failing tautness of the sentences, at what hour between midnight and daylight (she was a nocturnal worker) a particular passage had been written. It was with misgivings that I sent back my comments, for they were often drastic, and their implications were disagreeable to an ardent literary vanity. But she thanked me, unfailingly, without resentment, only clamouring to have the chapters back as quickly as possible, for time was always pressing on; and she used to set herself almost impossible deadlines which she scrupulously kept.

The demands she made on me, in fact, the impatience she showed, were mere shadows of the demands she made on herself, and these grew greater, more frenetic and obsessive, every year. She was constantly on the move, giving lectures in England or in France or in America, snatching time when she could to go to Dublin and see her mother whose support she felt as even more her responsibility than did the rest of her family. As early as May 1954 she was writing to me that she was just back from Dublin and had not had time even to undress between Monday and Thursday.

Her dealings with publishers were marked by the same intem-perate haste, braked only by the complexity of the publishing tangles into which she got herself, and her anxiety at once to have her own way and yet to convince herself that she had behaved with scrupulous fairness. Since the two aims were not always compatible, letters used to follow one another, each slightly quali-fying, while attempting to support, the arguments of its prede-cessor. Whenever she brought the ravelled skein to me for expert advice I privately congratulated myself I was not her publisher. 'I myself had always hoped to get settled with one publisher, who would have my interest at heart,' she once wrote to me. She could not see that for authors like herself, always playing one publisher off against another but unwilling to admit it, such a publisher was impossible. To one she felt she owed a loyalty, if not an option; but the loyalty would be contingent on his meeting her demands for more publicity or higher royalties. Another promised plenty of publicity but had charged her for excess corrections, something authors always resent, the more so if it is inescapably their own fault. Or she thought she could get a 20 per cent royalty from yet another, instead of the 15 per cent she had had on her previous book.

I would argue the pointlessness of such horse-trading, the inconsistency of professing loyalty without accepting that the very word implied some kind of sacrifice, the hollowness of a very high royalty which was inevitably fixed in relation to a number of copies which the book, already too highly priced, would never sell. It was useless. I was merely an expert with whom it was an extra luxury to talk about her problems, as a doctor is to a hypochondriac, a lawyer to someone with litigious mania, a confessor to a venial sinner with mortal scruples. Like most people she asked for advice only as a means of discoursing on her problems, not of solving them. And her determination to excel, the weak side of her sense of excellence, made it necessary for the vanity which was the hypertrophy of her self-respect to exact the highest royalty she could get, not for the money so much as for this external proof, as it were, that she was among the best of her kind.

It was this same desire for extrinsic evidence that she was among the 'best' that made her so proud of the recognition she received in France: France had in some ways replaced her father. There she did not wear trousers, still less the sailor's hat of the Marine Nationale. And it was the same with France in Oxford, the Maison Française. Its annual garden party was the true social centre of the summer term. Enid was so proud of her French decorations—first Chevalier of the Légion d'Honneur and later Officier—that she had the little red ribbon sewn even on her raincoats and pyjama jackets. But at the Maison Française she was always formally dressed and splendid in her doctoral gown. It was not until much champagne had been drunk—'only the English *pop* champagne corks, it's never done in France'—that the irrepressible gamine began to peek through the distinguished *femme de lettres*. Waving her glass in a hand which wore a ring that had once been Dean Swift's, she would announce with a pride which was only partly jocular that her rank in the Légion entitled her to a military salute at her funeral, or would reveal her wistful resentment that Maurice Bowra was a rung ahead on the ladder, being Commandeur to her Officier. 'After all, it's not as if Maurice really *knew* any French.'

The same spirit of emulation suffused her sense of herself as a Catholic and, though the severest thing she could say of someone was that he lacked '*ironie*', there was nothing ironic in her conception of herself. At a Catholic Chaplaincy party, while others were murmuring surprise at the presence of someone who never went to Mass, Enid herself was saying: 'Who are all these people? They don't look like real Catholics to me. They must be converts. I'm a Catholic, a real Catholic. I'm a bad Catholic.' She spoke as if the 'bad' Catholics were some very old, very special and exclusive sect. Nor would she readily countenance the accession of neophytes. She adjured a friend on the same occasion who confessed that he was a convert but thinking of lapsing, 'But you can't change your mind *twice*.'

At this party also she was heard to say to a man to whom she had been introduced: 'How long have you been a Catholic?' 'Thirty-seven years.' 'But I'm a cradle Catholic!' 'So am I.' 'Oh, I thought you were older than that.'

Another friend, a convert, asked her to be godmother to her child. Enid was flattered until the friend, a stern philosopher, went on: 'Of course, I shall want you to be in a state of grace.' So Enid did not become godmother.

Not that she was a mere egotist, egotistic though she could be, like most people of exceptional vitality. Such people, by the ardour and even the innocence of their interest in themselves and their almost objective wonder at the ceaseless drama of themselves, are like art, the enzyme which enables the rest of us to digest the workaday drabness of our own blank prose lives. We warm ourselves at the fire that burns them.

Besides, there were deep resources of sympathy, generosity, solicitude, in her, and she could bring the same energy to the help of others that, directed inwards, often made life difficult for herself. When I was in hospital in 1954 she sent my wife a few pounds with instructions that it was to be divided into the number of weeks I was to be laid up and thus produce a given amount of fruit each week. When she was in hospital herself with a malignant tumour in 1949, she had noticed that people sent lots of fruit and flowers the first week and after that did not bother. The incident was typical in many ways: the unselfish gesture working outwards from her own experience, the transposition of her lonely self into an imagination of me also feeling lonely and neglected; the wild fantasy that my wife would be as obsessively systematic as Enid herself in carrying out her directions; the impatience when her gift was not at once acknowledged, as she herself would have acknowledged it; the letters and telephone calls which followed to make sure her note and the money had not gone astray, and to ensure, one ungratefully felt, that a proper gratitude was not only felt but was formally expressed.

This was only one of the curious contradictions in her character, that concern for other people which could function only by her assuming that their identity was in some way co-ordinate with hers. The concern arose in part from, though in a sense it was created by, that fierce resolution to be wholly herself. It was this resolution that made her a 'character' and it could be sustained, along with her other incompatible desires, only by her contriving to be at once a public personality and a recluse. It meant that, although she had a multitude of friends—many of them much more patient and generous and solicitous than I ever was—she must also have no friends in the fullest sense, and in the sense that she sometimes felt she had none. It is a quality of many Irish people to be cheerfully gregarious and yet sometimes set on being solitary and sombre. Enid had this to a marked degree, and because she had no immediate family it was open to her to withdraw, to be free from the intimate domestic criticism which prevents us from forming too much our own standard of what is and should be. It went with that other contradiction in her—*elle raisonne toujours*—that inability to admit that she was ever in the wrong, or at least to admit it without such qualifications as to show that she was really in the right; an inability which, if consistently carried through, would have eliminated the need to argue at all but which in her case could not be consistent. For, as a stubborn individual, she was sure she was right but, to conciliate her fantasy of herself as an objectively rational person and to carry out her role as a member of society, she had to get others to concede she was right.

But time was pressing on and time, never for long anyone's ally, was inexorably becoming her enemy. In the early sixties she seemed to grow more argumentative, more petulant, to be more conscious of stress. Things that might have been expected to please her had a way of turning out wrong, of disappointing. The College wanted her portrait painted, for example, and this was a satisfaction to her; for the College was part of her life, a second family to love and quarrel with and love again, a famous institution with which she was proud to identify. But she grudged the time lost in frequent visits to London for sittings, time taken from her work—'And the last time I was there he spent a whole day painting one ear-ring, a whole day, and it wasn't one of my best ear-rings either.' Nor in the end was she very happy with the result. She was not one of those whom any painter with a vision of his own could satisfy: the self she saw was something she had created but so was the self who saw it; whereas the painter, however penetrating his eye and whatever his empathy, saw someone other.

About this time, too, she began to have fits of coughing, vaguely disturbing bronchial troubles, frequent temperatures. Till now we had always regarded a 'temperature' of Enid's as the nearest formula she would grant herself for a hangover, a euphemism for a weakness she could not otherwise acknowledge. But the temperatures began to lose their inverted commas, became too marked, too tenacious, and too recurrent. By 1964 it was clear enough from her copious but varying versions of the doctor's opinion that there really was something seriously the matter with her lungs.

So, when she was invited to Cape Town as a visiting professor, medical advice was rather against it, though not absolutely. She decided to go, never able to resist the feeling that she was wanted, that there was another field to conquer, and always emulous of the title and status of Professor. She found the work far more exacting than she expected, partly because of her own conscientiousness but partly because she was really ill. The doctors in Cape Town did their best but were as baffled for diagnosis as those of Oxford, or as reticent. Various possibilities were mooted and excluded; for example, early tubercles 'which sound like new potatoes', as she wrote to me. 'All the week, before I saw the doctor here, I was looking at my face for signs of deterioration. Of course I thought I looked tired, but then I am tired.'

She had turned her attention to Flaubert and she concluded that there was enough new material to make a biography worth while. When she came back in September 1964 she decided to take a term off and work on the book. From now onwards she set her mind on finishing this book, whatever the odds. Watching her when she was talking to no one and so not animated, and when she was unaware of being observed, you could see that she was sinking visibly into age and gloom and the heart went out to the courage in her that made her resolute to go on, to work come what may.

The doctors, she said, had decided that she had cancer in both lungs. She determined that she would try to go on living as normal a life as possible for as long as possible, letting her friends know that she was ill but making every effort to prevent this becoming a nuisance to them or interfering with friendship. In *A Lady's Child* she had written—then in the prime of her life and powers, though the book reads as if it were written by a very young woman, so immediate and recent seems the world it re-creates—against *amor fati*, against resignation, against acquiescence in despair. 'It cannot be right for adult spirits to weep and to grow despairing over the broken toys of childhood and the fading of the fairylands.' She had refused then to take a defeatist view of life. 'Life has been for me like a Chinese box. Inside that box is another, inside yet another, and so forth, for ever and ever world without end, it seems to me. Each box is a little smaller than the previous one, but each is as lovely as, in some ways lovelier than, the one which contained it. Shall I ever reach the empty centre where there is no box to be found, no place for a box? I do not believe it. Perhaps the centre is solid platinum, a cube of incorruptible platinum waiting for me to find it.'

It is easy to write with such spirit against the inevitable when one is in one's middle prime, less easy when the inevitable is at one's elbow. But something of that steady remembering of one's last day that a Catholic training inculcates, or used to, was a constant with Enid. Before there had been any question of a mortal illness she had once said to me, apropos of I have forgotten what, 'Never a day passes without my thinking of death.' She spoke with such simplicity that I readily believed her; was indeed to wish that I didn't believe her since the saying came back, and comes back, so often into my own mind that it is virtually true for me also. And who knows whether, to be fair, we ought not to admit, those of us who were brought up by religion in the constant reminder of the presence of death and the vastness of eternity, whatever our subsequent faith or lack of it, that such early conditioning acts as a stiffener when the imminence of oblivion begins to menace and overshadow our sunny amnesia, the skilled forgetfulness which enables us like Johnson's failed philosopher to keep cheerful?

Enid, then, with all that backbone and pride of hers, bent herself now to a task outside herself, to work, the best resource of those who have repudiated prayer. Only strong temptations could now distract her but, if they were strong enough, she still had the reserves to rise to them. Thus she set off gallantly in May 1965 to be *intronisée* as Chevalier du Tastevin in the Clos-Vougeot, a ceremony that with a dinner was to last from afternoon till midnight, and daunted even the stout-hearted Felix Markham who escorted her and concealed his concern lest she fail to survive.

She survived to return and display the trophies of her certificate and insignia one Saturday in the pub, as pleased as a child; this though the doctors were now allowing her the expectation of no more than six months of life, and that only with the most rigorous and exacting treatments. She decided she must resign her Readership and her College Fellowship, representing this to herself and to us as heroic sacrifice, though she knew then as we know now that the age limit would in any case soon have made retirement inevitable. For she guarded the year of her birth as a close secret, perhaps even from herself, she who remembered with punctual card the birthdays of everyone. Even to me, who had long since written at her own suggestion her *Times* obituary, she would never reveal the essential date.

Inevitable or not, the severance from the stage of action was painful to her, and especially ceasing to be an active Fellow of Somerville, the College with which her association went back so far. But all must now give way to Flaubert, and there was a fitness in its being Flaubert, who had sacrificed himself to his art.

Her friends, severally and in combination, were able to wring some concessions from her. She was persuaded to try to live more comfortably when in Paris, to remember that she was no longer a *pique-assiette*, a poor student who must practise every petty economy. It wasn't easy, for she had built into the structure of her personality the habit of being austere, frugal, parsimonious even, in her private life. The house in Walton Street to which she had lately moved, after a fierce rear-guard battle against the University authorities who wanted to convert her flat to bureaucratic purposes, was furnished even more splendidly; but the beautiful objects it contained had all in their time been bargains. The house itself she had been enabled to purchase with financial help from admiring American friends. It had a kitchen fitted out with every kind of accessory, pampered as a racehorse and flaunting her colours, red and blue. It was a kitchen of which Lizzie, the family cook of Enid's girlhood, would have been proud. I doubt whether Enid, alone in it, ever produced anything more elaborate than a boiled egg.

There was a danger that if one undermined this spartan frugality of hers one would imperil the whole fabric of her personality, the courage and self-sacrifice, the dedication to work, of which it was part. None the less we managed to temper the self-chastener in her a little. She was persuaded to have herself driven to and from the airport when she travelled, even if she could not be persuaded against the exhausting journeys themselves; and so she no longer went by train and bus to Heathrow, walking the final distance through the tunnel and trundling her battered luggage before her.

By this time we had moved our Saturday mornings, first to the Horse and Jockey, and finally to the Victoria Arms. Enid complained that the seats in this last pub were too high for her short legs. So a friend bought a Victorian footstool which was fetched out from behind the bar whenever she arrived. And we tried to arrange for someone to bring her by car and take her back to Somerville for lunch. Even so, she walked whenever she could, and I often overtook her as I came from work, making her way laboriously, pausing for breath sometimes while pretending to look in a shop window.

But she came less regularly. Small typed notes would tell me that she had had to keep another appointment or, increasingly often, that she was too unwell to come out. I tried to persuade her not to bother to write—these were casual gatherings and no one but Enid would have bothered—but her punctilio was too strong. When she did come, we would hear her shoving at the door, so light to us and so heavy to her. One of us would jump up to hold it open. Panting for breath, very light and very frail, she would come in and sit down. She would give that series of gasping sighs now habitual with her. The stool would be brought, and Irish and soda. Watching her covertly, I was reminded of a bird, fearful in a hand enclosing it.

'You look much better,' I would say, in an aside. 'I don't know why you say that, when I feel so terrible. Everyone keeps saying things like that. They don't know how I feel.' Indignant, she was herself, and transition to her genial company-loving self was possible. She became animated and ready to argue and to gossip, for a little while forgetful of the implacable enemy, the hand that held her enclosed. I would draw her on to talk of her *Flaubert*.

In spite of the Bibliothèque Nationale, where the only fresh air was a fierce draught from the door and where she never failed to catch a cold, in spite of the long, complicated journeys to Chantilly where the library was open only twice a year for ten days each time, in spite of that fear of death which can make all art seem pointless, she managed to finish the first volume of the *Flaubert*. In August 1966 she gave a party for a few intimates to celebrate its conclusion. It became clear that she now dared to hope, if not to expect, that she would live to finish the second volume.

This was the year of another election to the Chair of Poetry. At the previous election in 1961, against our advice she had stood in a four-cornered contest from which Robert Graves had emerged top of the poll and Enid herself last. I had charged her with inconsistency in standing at all, since she was not a poet. She rationalized her position somehow, but her unacknowledged reason was probably an intense desire to be a Professor at Oxford. She had failed to get the Chair of French Literature in 1949, and the disappointment still rankled. She had found some consolation in visiting professorships abroad, even though at Berkeley she claimed that she had to do so much lecturing that she ran out of knowledge and had to spend long hours in the library acquiring more. She had taught at Seattle and, most enjoyable of all, at Hollins College, Virginia, where she had been made much of and formed lasting friendships. But these were peripheral, proconsulships only. She still longed to be consul in Rome.

Now in 1966 she did not stand again for the Chair of Poetry because she was unwell. But if she could not be a king she still could not relinquish trying to be a kingmaker. Friends of ours had indicated to her at a party that they intended to nominate Robert Lowell and at the time she seemed to think it a good idea. Shortly afterwards, however, she herself nominated Edmund Blunden. We protested that Lowell was her natural candidate, a poet still young and writing poetry, that Blunden's time was past. She replied that she owed her support to Blunden because in 1951 he had stood down in favour of her candidate, Day-Lewis. She did not say, perhaps did not realize, that the real objection to Lowell was that someone else had thought of him first. So she put her remaining strength into the fray, and the University, for reasons not necessarily the same as hers, elected Blunden.

That feat performed and the distraction over, and cheered also by the award of a C.B.E. in the New Year honours for 1967, she pushed on with the second Flaubert volume. Her health now seemed to have paused upon a plateau—she did not regain strength but no longer lost it so rapidly. On special occasions, such as the grand luncheon given her in London by representatives of Hollins College with a special medal to honour her and link her with its 125th anniversary, she was able to blaze up with something of her former fire. Soon proofs of her first Flaubert volume were coming in and she asked me to read a set—but so urgent were her pleas for speed that I was not able to do much with them.

And she was still driven to overtax what strength she still disposed of. In black mid-December she was off to get an honorary degree at Aix-en-Provence. Nor could she resist an invitation to a visiting professorship at Columbia University for the first semester of 1968. But Columbia, in a bitter winter with a temperature so severe that she once fainted with the cold, was not Hollins College. New York was remote and impersonal, America was in upheaval with revolt against authority and the Vietnam war. Columbia was a trouble spot and she was distressed by the outrages then taking place. Her teaching kept her busy ten hours a day, there was no time to spare for Flaubert, and her expenses ran close on her income. She claimed to have ended by living on bananas.

Once at least she escaped into social life, a party given by a friend of ours in Greenwich Village. Standing against the wall in her jacket and trousers, red and blue, she was a figure of mark, even in that place and time. She was in full discourse, her glass constantly replenished and as constantly emptied by sips or by gesture, the wine descending like the rain impartially on just and unjust. Something was troubling a girl at her feet, even apart from perplexity about Enid and what she was saying. In the brief moments when Enid stopped talking to take a sip, the girl kept murmuring, 'Pardon me.' Enid talked on. The glass emphasized a new point. The girl got wetter. At last she could bear it no longer. 'Pardon me,' she said, rather loudly, 'but you're standing on my hand.' Uninterrupted Enid lifted her foot and her captive withdrew, nursing her hand, to a drier spot.

But such brighter moments were few, and she was tired and chastened when she came back to Oxford in July. I did not have the heart to repeat the arguments I had used before she went: that it was folly to wear herself out on these pointless excursions: she would still have had the spirit to persist she was in the right. In

October I heard that she had been talking of standing for the Chair of Poetry, now that Blunden had retired from it on grounds of health. She said nothing of this to me. No doubt she knew what I would say and was no longer ready to cope with the argument she would once have courted. So I watched in silence when in due course she was nominated and the inevitable ballyhoo followed. This time, fortunately, she was more discreet with the Press, but it was painful for her friends who believed that she was bound to be defeated. Roy Fuller would in fact have been my own preference but I could not bring myself to vote against Enid and so did not vote at all. Fuller won.

Silence on this subject continued between us until Christmas. She could no longer walk round Oxford delivering her own Christmas cards to save postage, and the whole business of preparing the seven hundred she usually sent, though not at all abated, must have been a weariness to her. But she still loved the excitement. 'I shall miss Christmas terribly whenever you decide not to have it,' she had written to us—a typical disguised appeal that we should continue to have it and continue to invite her. This particular Christmas of 1968, as it happened, we dined with friends who, knowing our ritual obligation, invited Enid also. I seized a moment after dinner to mention the election, incautiously hoping to make my own attitude intelligible. But she was still sore and resentful and we were both relieved to be interrupted.

In the old days Joyce Cary had always given a party at which he would see in the New Year with his friends. Since his death in 1957 Enid had carried on the custom. After the party for the New Year of 1969 I wrote to thank her. She replied, deprecating my rash suggestion that she had looked well and saying that she had in fact been very unwell and feverish with a temperature of 102°. 'I have been making good New Year's resolutions and am trying to tidy up my life. I am going to sacrifice everything to getting on with my work and so am going to cut out inessentials. I have decided not to go every week to the Victoria Arms, but only intermittently until I finish my work.' I recognized the very accent, the resolve to face the truth however sombre, that recurs so often in the later letters of Katherine Mansfield.

Later in the month, sending me her centenary lecture on Baudelaire given at Nice, she returned to the election over which she
still brooded. 'If one learns anything from education it is to be
detached and to separate friendship, affection and love from political considerations.' I smiled—this was something Enid aspired
to learn perhaps, but had not really learnt. Still, she was trying to
reassure me that she was not hurt because I was not one of those
who supported her for the Chair of Poetry and recognized that I
had special reasons. She went on to say how disappointed she was
in those friends and colleagues who had shown no sympathy with
her and in the seven weeks between nomination and election had
not even mentioned the subject. 'I have a great many dear friends
but, like a woman with a lot of children, I did not want to spare
any of them.' It was like her not to have seen the ambiguity of
that 'spare'. She didn't regret not having been elected, she went
on, as it would have complicated her life and her health was not
good. She had stood only because Robert Graves pressed her to
do so and she was glad because the election had shown her how
many people wished her well. But she did regret that in some
close friends she had found she could not count on human sympathy, understanding, and kindness. 'But I must not regret it too
much as I have always claimed that I preferred the vision of truth
to illusion.' Again I smiled, and sadly, because I felt that I too had
been lacking by her standards; and also because Enid so little
realized that her valiant 'vision of truth' must, like everyone else's
truths, be tainted by the illusion she deplored, since the components of our vision, our truth, must always derive from the
world of appearances and be selected and combined by our own
subjective choice.

In any case this note of resignation was more willed than real.
The spirit of combat was still strong in her. Thus she found time
and energy for a tussle with the *Spectator*. 'I got fun out of it,' she
wrote in sending me the dossier for my delectation and speedy
return, 'and I wrote ten letters, and I imagine each of them
infuriated the editor more than the last.' She still came fairly often
to join us on Saturdays and was still able to divert us and herself
with intricate details of how she had discomfited the adversaries

who were as necessary to her for enjoyment as friends were, while she breathed. At such moments it was easy to forget she was very ill. There were others when it was not. I remember meeting her on a cold spring day that year, seeing her before she saw me. She was creeping slowly and painfully along Little Clarendon Street, looking terribly forlorn and resting against each pillar of the arcade as she reached it. I took her arm and asked if I could help. Almost in tears she explained that coming back from College she had lost some note or other—itself of no great importance to anyone except Enid. So she was retracing her steps from home to College in the hope of finding it. I persuaded her to give up the search and come home.

In July my wife and I went off to New Zealand. When we came back in September Enid was just returned from Paris and apologized for not having sent a note of welcome for our homecoming. Paris had been miserable and cold. Each day she longed to be home in Oxford. Often she had to go to bed at six in the evening. 'It is not worth being in Paris for that.' Christmas came racing on and afterwards there was the usual punctilious note of thanks 'for the wonderful party for Christmas day, wonderful food and fabulous wine'. I was struck by remorse. Dinner had been at midday, because of small grandchildren, and afterwards Enid, across spilling brandy, had recklessly extolled Flaubert as a novelist over Tolstoy, insistent and repetitive, inaccessible to counter-argument. Bored, I had fallen asleep.

For her party that New Year's Eve, she summoned herself up once more, vivid and hectic ghost of her former self in a brilliant Chinese mandarin gown; but each year now, as I heard the bells ringing in the New Year and the sirens shrieking and the railway engines hooting, I remembered friends who had not lived to see another year begin and I wondered whether for Enid this one would be the last.

In February she grew worse and was put on more powerful drugs. None the less, the second Flaubert volume finished, she had begun to think of writing a book on Laforgue, though doubting whether she would live to do it. 'I'm full of ideas of all sorts of things, which will probably never be done. It is just like a

woman reaching non child-bearing age, who most easily conceives.' The analogy was odd but one could see what she meant;
and in the life of a writer death is the only menopause. She became
preoccupied with the obscure fate of Laforgue's English wife.
'Poor little Leah Lee, the wife of one of the most famous poets in
France in the nineteenth century, is as if she had never existed.'
The work to be done on Laforgue would take five years. 'I talk
glibly of five years when it often seems impossible that I should
go on living for five years as I am now.'

On 3 April Robert Shackleton gave a luncheon party in Brasenose for an Irish poet, Desmond O'Grady. My wife and I arrived
a little late for the drinks beforehand. Enid was sitting in an armchair in the far corner of that beautifully book-lined room, dressed
in her more formal manner, wearing a skirt. As always, she had
brightened up for a party and she seemed full of animation. We
talked while we waited for the guests still to come. Maurice
Bowra was the last to arrive. He greeted his host and then hastened
towards Enid. 'And how are you, Enid? Still dying?' I froze for a
moment but everyone laughed, Enid as loud as any. For the time
being the bold question seemed to dispel its possibility.

We ate then, Enid praising the food and the wine and doing
justice to both. Afterwards we gave her a lift in our taxi as far as
her house in Walton Street. I got out to see her to the door. She
turned and looked back to thank us and to say goodbye. The
animation was departing from her face, the weariness returning.
Inside, she would be alone. She took out her keys. It was to be the
last time we saw her.

The following Friday she wrote to apologize for not being able
to join us next day in the pub. Her doctor would not let her go
out. She hoped to see us the Saturday after. That Saturday came
and there was another, briefer note, 'My doctor won't allow it.
I've been very ill all the week. I'm very sorry.'

She had not expressed, this time, the hope of another Saturday.
I was worried, that Friday 17 April, after getting her note. I rang
and asked her if she would like me to come and see her that night
or next morning. Usually she would have welcomed the suggestion. But she thanked me and said she was too tired. As she put

down the receiver I heard her give a heavy sigh, a sigh of relinquishment.

In the night of the following Tuesday she had a massive heart attack. She had agreed after long persuasion to be taken to hospital next day rather than go on living alone and so seriously ill. But in the morning there was no reply when a Somerville friend knocked at her door. She was found dead on the landing of her stair, where she had fallen, having died on her feet. She had reached the last centre of the Chinese box and found, perhaps, the cube of incorruptible platinum.

Five Windows Darken

Joyce Cary

Self-portrait, 1955

5
Five Windows Darken

JOYCE CARY
(1888-1957)

> Five windows light the caverned man.
> WILLIAM BLAKE

JOYCE CARY was a name to my wife and me long before we ever met him. In that splendid summer of 1940 a month or so before the German breakthrough, my wife was staying at Rhodes House in Oxford with the Warden, C. K. Allen, and his wife Dorothy. They had insisted she be their guest until her baby was due and had arranged a bed for her in the maternity wing of the Radcliffe. I was a cadet at 168 O.C.T.U. in North Camp and came up to Rhodes House for week-ends whenever I could get leave.

There was much talk on these occasions of a man named Cary. He and C.K. were both Air Raid Wardens and shared an A.R.P. post. He was a fascinating conversationalist, apparently, and was working on a novel with a woman as central character—no doubt *Herself Surprised*. He was finding it difficult, he told Dorothy, to write about a woman from the inside and was always bombarding her with questions: how did she, as a woman, feel about this, that, and the other.

He had published several novels already, it seemed, though I don't recall that the Allens had ever read any of them, and they certainly were not known to us, who counted ourselves well-read in contemporary fiction.

Our eldest daughter was born not long afterwards and the chances of war took us away from Oxford. I went off to the Middle East and the name of Joyce Cary dropped out of my mind until I came home on leave in 1943. My wife, now in Bristol, had just read *Herself Surprised* and was full of her discovery of a great new writer. Such enthusiasm is usually counter-productive and I began the novel with scepticism. Afterwards, I was heard to say to friends: 'I have discovered a great new writer.' We went on to devour *To Be a Pilgrim* which had been published the year before.

At the end of the war and 1945 we came, now a family of two daughters with a third due shortly, back to Oxford and my first civilian job. Meanwhile *The Horse's Mouth* had been published in 1944. So far as the rest of the world was concerned there was no longer any question of 'discovery', for these three novels had made Cary famous. He was still living in Oxford, we gathered, but we were too diffident to seek him out. It was through Walter Allen this time, not C.K., that we first met him and his wife Trudy. For Cary and I were both then published by Michael Joseph and Walter not only published with him also but was his fiction reader.

My pemmican diary, fitfully kept, notes that the meeting with Cary took place on 30 August 1947, and that there was something 'birdishly alert' about him. We discussed his early friendship with Middleton Murry when the two of them were undergraduates together. I asked him about Katherine Mansfield. He had not liked her, had thought her hard, selfish, and a little sordid, then. Later, he realized he had been wrong. I suggested she must have lacked intellectual rigour or she would never have been taken in by Gurdjieff and Fontainebleau. He defended her: she was 'looking for the answer'. My diary notes also that he said, as a statement of simple fact and not from arrogance, 'Of course, I don't read new novels much. I only read masterpieces.'

Before long my wife met the Carys also and from time to time we saw them at parties or entertained one another to dinner. Our relations became friendly though they were our seniors by a quarter of a century. For most people in their late fifties as Cary was then, with a close and happy family life, four grown-up sons often coming back home on visits, a busy working routine and an already wide range of friends, it is not easy to find time and energy for new friendships, especially with people of another generation, a different past and different codes of living. But Joyce was always open to new experience, new people, always alive and interested, ready to give and ready to listen. He and Trudy were deeply attached to each other but it was an attachment that did not exclude, did not obtrude. Their house in Parks Road had a warmth in which a visitor could bask.

Their drawing-room was full of pictures, some painted by Joyce himself. These were all of his family—his wife playing the cello, his sons as children playing with their toys. There was an almost hieratic stiffness in the execution. They were clearly the work of a man who had talent and was well grounded in the rules of his craft. One could see that Gulley Jimson's creator had not written as an amateur but was speaking from the horse's mouth. One sensed too, though, why he had abandoned paint for words, a freer medium for one who abounded in life, and who wanted to say something more explicit than paint would allow.

It was not till after his death that I found confirmation of this in *Art and Reality* (1958). 'Painters, sculptors, architects and composers do not intuit a moral real, or attempt to express it. They are dealing entirely with sensuous reality in colour, sound and form, and their works are aimed in the first place only at a sensuous reaction. This does not exclude a moral effect. There is certainly a connection between purely sensuous reality and emotional consequences.' But 'the arts of music, painting and sculpture do not take a moral problem as their theme and meaning; whereas all the written arts, except the purely factual, do nothing else.' The writer 'creates for us a whole of meaning which is essentially moral' and 'we judge the truth of his work by its revelation of a moral real' even if the emphasis and the angle are peculiar to the individual writer. And the reason that the novelist ultimately treats a moral problem is that he is creating a world of action and must therefore deal with motive, with morality. 'All novels are concerned from first to last with morality.' It was because Joyce Cary was a moralist that he became a novelist.

Though the art of words, then, had become his finally chosen art, his interest in the other arts had remained very lively as other pictures in his drawing-room besides his own attested. And there was a piano, too, for it was a musical house. His wife was an accomplished cellist, his son Tristram a composer, his son Peter a fine pianist, and his son Michael made harpsichords. And the books that filled the shelves ranged far more widely than fiction.

Conspicuous among the furniture was a sea captain's mahogany chest which Joyce had had converted to a drinks cabinet—he was a great man for planning cupboards and shelves all over the house and during the war he had made kitchen furniture for the refugees whom he then housed in the attic storey. The carpets and rugs were themselves fine things. The windows looked out across to the University Parks and in the room there were always flowers.

A room, then, at once the background and the cast—wormcast, he would have said—of a writer, a man of taste, a man who liked light and books and company. As from the fossilized track of a trilobite, you would have been able to infer from the room alone the nature of those who lived in it, people for whom the family, society, existed.

In Joyce himself there was obvious, from the earliest acquaintance, warmth of character, quickness of response; an intelligence as eager in general ideas as in observation of persons and of *faits divers*, but without cloudiness in the one or malice in the other. It would soon be evident to anyone that he, like Katherine Mansfield, had long been 'looking for the answer'; that he thought he had found it, in general terms, but knew that at best the 'answer' was something that had to be sought and found afresh for any particular problem or situation. Moral theory was one thing, its application another. So that, although he loved argument, he did not argue for victory or out of egotism but always with an engaging eagerness and always from the angle of his own convictions, never taking authority on trust, though recognizing and praising knowledge, authenticity.

This combination of inner certainty and passion for finding out the truth in all the peculiarity of the specific case evoked a like response in others, disarming the arrogant or pretentious, and turning polemic into a common inquiry. And his relish for the quiddities and character of others, together with his great natural courtesy, enabled him to listen and to stimulate his *vis-à-vis* by his enjoyment.

Our friendship did not all at once ripen into intimacy. These were busy years for both of us. I was finishing my third novel, seeing a book of short stories through the press, preparing the groundwork for an official history of the battle of Crete, working for my living by day in the Clarendon Press and, as often as not, dining out of an evening in one college or another, partly for pleasure and partly propelled by the outward ripples of official duty. Joyce himself was deep in the writing of *A Fearful Joy* and had many other interests and obligations.

By the time I knew him he had developed a steady pattern of working which remained basically the same for the rest of his life in spite of the modifications imposed in later years by failing health. He was a light sleeper and usually awoke about four in the morning. He would then lie in bed thinking about new novels to write or about the book on which he was at the moment concentrating. He would scribble notes of any good points that struck him and, as he had a remarkable capacity for holding in his mind the general design of what he was doing, he could contemplate the whole thing as a painter might study an unfinished canvas, comparing it with the more or less complete picture in his mind to which it ought eventually, when finished, to approximate.

On 'lucky days' he might get a little further sleep before getting up at 7.30. After breakfast he would deal with his correspondence and then go upstairs to his study in the attic, while his wife or, later, his secretary typed the letters he had dictated or tried to decipher the more or less illegible manuscript he had written the day before.

Over his desk in the attic was a shelf of twelve compartments which he had designed for holding the files of the novel on which he was at work. Each chapter had its own file. But before embarking on a narrative text at all he would write notes about his possible theme and the characters who were to enact it. Where place was important he would draw plans of the house or scene and these too would have their special folders.

Partly because writing was his profession and to that extent his time was his own, partly because he was naturally so prolific, he might make any number of starts, trying to discover what line marched best with his basic theme, trying to isolate it. Once he had made up his mind he would attempt to get down on paper the crucial scene, wherever it might come in the finished novel— beginning, middle, or end. From there he would go on to write different parts of the book as he felt ready for them, or as one scene seized his imagination rather than another. He worked like a painter at whatever part of the canvas seemed to need development in relation to the rest and as the various parts built up he would be working on them all as it were simultaneously.

Sometimes he would find his theme or his plot dividing and sub-dividing, or one of the characters would insist on grabbing the initiative and Joyce would indulge him while he obstinately developed beyond the role originally assigned to him. When this happened Joyce would follow the new path or the changed character for a certain distance before deciding whether this was the true way ahead or how far the new development could be contained within the broad framework that the basic theme and over-all intention required. If the trail proved to be a false way out of the maze or the mutinous character grew out of control, Joyce would lop off the branch at its divergence from the main stem and put it away, perhaps to become the germ of some future novel or story, and would return to the main line.

So he worked, proliferating and yet all the time narrowing as the exigencies of the choices made compelled him to hew ever closer to the form. At the end the novel emerged, like a completed life, all possibility of further choice forgone. Yet before that could happen and while the process of discard was still incomplete he was usually left with a baggy monster which had to be savagely cut and put together again or 'jointed up' as he called it, and tailored, whatever the wastage, to the most concise and swiftly moving form consistent with his original 'intuition'.

In January 1948 I must have written something to him about *The Horse's Mouth* and *Mr. Johnson*. For I find him replying on 2 February: 'The Jimson-Johnson parallel is fundamental. Both are men of imagination and only such men can overcome the injustice of life. Jimson's fear of hating anybody because hatred will kill his art is of course beyond Johnson—he lives in the present (and in the present tense) like a child simply forgetting to hate. I'll look at that time sequence you mention. I am a free cutter and careless corrector. The cuts often break up my time schedule and I forget to change them—often a complex job.

'I am cutting now—and nearly off my head with the job. I enjoyed our evening. When the pressure relaxes a bit we'll have another.' And he adds a postscript. 'It was good of you to write— I know what trouble it is for a busy man.'

The 'injustice of life' is a characteristic phrase, corresponding to something which he felt profoundly. Elsewhere he recalls: 'To us, from earliest childhood, in England or Ireland, the fundamental injustice of things, the cruelty of blind fate, were as natural as the air we breathed.' But it was important both to realize the exis-tence of that injustice and to accept it for oneself, even if one tried to ameliorate it for others. It was because of that injustice that the hatred which Gulley so much feared was possible at all, and Joyce himself felt the same need to avoid hating. Grief he could not avoid but he knew it also could be the enemy of his art and this was one ingredient of his willed stoicism in the troubles he had already endured and those, much worse, that were still to come.

My diary records a meeting on 12 April that year. 'I notice certain stories and generalizations seem to recur from previous conversations; presumably the symbols and landmark summaries that have a special significance for him as he looks back. And the same metaphors occur and recur when he speaks of his own work: "the lump", "plastic", "digging", "vein", "I don't know what I've got yet". A man of very definite judgements who keeps his self-confidence immune by having little to do with contemporary critics and not exposing his sensibility to their acids.'

I was right to pick on these words. Cary regarded his experience as a mine, a gross mass of rock, from which an ore had to be extracted and refined and then moulded into a particular shape. And he found the task so engrossing that he did not wish to be distracted, except when he himself was ready to leave the face, to get some air or because the problem could only be solved away from the actual workings. In such a state he would say, like Gulley Jimson, that he was 'stuck' and he would go out for a rapid walk in the University Parks or in the Oxford streets, revolving his problem and drawing on the prodigious resources of his invention. Close friends could pass within feet of him and not be recognized though, when outwardly alert and not inwardly intent, he was a close observer of everything external. His concentration was so intense as to be almost trancelike. If you wanted him to become aware of your existence you had to stop and wave your arms and call his name before a smile of recognition and an outward light would appear upon his face.

At other times he would break shift because his stint was for the moment done, the problem solved or shelved, and he felt he needed company or social distraction. This happened more often after Trudy's death. While she was alive she provided him with most of the society he needed emotionally. It was she, also, who protected him from the wrong sort of distraction, including the critics and their acids. As Gulley avoided hatred, and for the same reasons, Joyce avoided reading most of the reviews of his work and the exasperation of finding himself yet again wrongly understood. Trudy read them for him and screened out anything she thought he might find useful or interesting.

Similarly, out of a desire not to be involved in sterile arguments and the quarrels of coteries, he avoided the literary world of London. There may, here, have been a residue of disillusionment from earlier days when, in 1912, returning to London after long absence in the Balkan war and eager for friends to talk to, he had called on the Murrys and been told they were not at home, though the house above was loud with the noise of a literary party.

He did make an occasional sally, however, and once went to take tea with Ivy Compton-Burnett, one of the few contemporary novelists whom he admired. They inquired of each other about their next books and Joyce launched into an explanation of how his current novel was not quite as he wanted but there seemed no way of doing any more to it. 'I see,' his hostess said, passing him the jam, 'you mean it has jelled.' Joyce was very pleased with the homely metaphor, so like one of his own, or of Sara Monday's, and adopted it thenceforward.

Trudy, it sometimes seemed to us, knew more of Joyce's creative processes than he did himself. One evening someone was relating a scrape of Dylan Thomas's. He had been lent a flat, it was said, and being broke had gradually pawned everything until only the silver was left. He had set it out on the hall table and begun to clean it before taking it to pawn also. His hosts unexpectedly returned. 'How thoughtful of you to have cleaned the silver for us. You shouldn't have bothered.' Trudy shot a mischievous glance at Joyce and he looked uncomfortable. We all thought of Pinto in *A House of Children*, similarly overtaken; and of Gulley's outrageous adventures in the Beeders' flat. Whether Joyce had already heard this anecdote when he was writing his novel or whether the story itself is true hardly matters; for Joyce did not have to go direct to the actual, given his fertility of invention.

That year, 1948, was the beginning of a time of troubles for Joyce and his family. Trudy became seriously ill. On 25 April, according to a diary of Joyce's, she told him she had a lump in her breast. Her doctor advised immediate action and Joyce went next day to see his brother-in-law Heneage Ogilvie, a distinguished surgeon at Guy's Hospital, and make arrangements. The entry for the following day reads:

1948 April 27. Today when I came back from London and went to Trudy I still felt confused with this frightful and unexpected blow. As T. said 'It's like a dream but now we know we're not going to wake up.'

What is strange is that I got no pleasure, in walking through the Parks and looking at the new leaves on the trees, at the buttercups which are just opening in crowds among the bright green new grass. I used to think that looking at nature would always give me consolation in misery, but it did not do so today. The only thing that gave me

comfort was simply a feeling for other people in misfortune and their
need of love. I was made to feel, I suppose, for the first time the
absolute need of love to make life possible, and the continuous everlast-
ing presence of love in the world. And so the fearful bitterness of this
danger to T. and all our memories together was mixed with the sense
of something that can survive any loss, the power to love.

Trudy had her operation almost at once and when she was well
enough to travel Joyce took her on holiday to Switzerland and
the same hotels and places they had visited when they were young.
His novels were having some success now in the United States
and he was desperately anxious that she should live to enjoy the
success with him, and the easier circumstances it promised to
bring. But no cherishing, no reliving of a past when they were
young and struggling and happy, could arrest the progress of the
disease. When they came back to Oxford she was more and more
confined to the house and in need of constant care. When I
returned at the end of September from New Zealand where I had
been talking to old soldiers about the battle of Crete I found that
life at Parks Road, in spite of surface serenity, had a sombre
undertone. We went there sometimes to dinner parties and they
came now and then to us. Trudy was courageous and cheerful
but after a time any formal entertaining became impossible for her.

Sometimes, in his distress, Joyce would feel forced to emerge
and seek relief and distraction through his friends. Our daughters,
the youngest then three and the oldest eight, became important
to him. He listened to children with two levels of attention—one,
the attention due to any other human being but especially to those
young and needing security and love; and the other, the attention
one might give to an oracle, to a being still young enough to have
the wisdom of innocence. Nothing delighted him more than
the occasional saying which came out of their graver, more
metaphysical moods: 'How can God's face see everything if his
face is always in the same place?' 'I like pink and red and mauve
and purple best but next year I hope to like green best too.'
'Where was I before I was born, Mummy?' 'You were inside me.'
'But before that?' 'You weren't anywhere, dear.' 'Where am I
now?'

In February 1949 Gerald Wilde, the painter, came to live in Oxford where a friend of ours, Wendy Campbell Purdie, gave him free board and lodging so as to help him recover his health and paint. About a month later a crowd of us came back from a sherry party in Somerville to our house, where Joyce had arranged to join us for coffee. It was getting late when suddenly Gerald appeared. Joyce had never met him and was sufficiently startled by Gerald to remember the meeting long afterwards. Gerald was 'a figure strange even in that gathering place of poets and professors; of dreamers in all dimensions'.

Gerald, whose medium had never been words, was incoherent with excitement at meeting the creator of Gulley Jimson; for he himself had long been nicknamed the Gulley Jimson of Soho, though the differences between him and Gulley were at least as marked as the resemblances, themselves undeniable and superficially the most obvious. He rushed forward now with the mixed intention of shaking Joyce's hand and embracing Enid Starkie. He managed neither but overturned a table of glasses and bottles with a tremendous crash and splashing.

Though he does not say so in his account of the meeting, published in *Nimbus* in 1955, the encounter may have been a shock for Joyce in another way. He would have seen quickly enough the sense in which Gerald was an incarnation of Gulley, and here was another case of reality imitating art. But it would not have needed that specific responsibility to bring out Joyce's unfailing kindness and sympathy for a fellow-artist in need of help. Before long he was buying pictures from Gerald, some of the finest he painted in what turned out to be a prolific period. He lent Gerald money also for paints, but when he found that the money was being spent before it reached the paint shop in Broad Street he opened an account there so that Gerald could buy paints up to a given amount each week without actually having to handle money; for, as Gerald used to tell us proudly, Jung once told a psychoanalyst friend who had described the painter to him that Gerald was a man for whom money was 'poison'.

A Fearful Joy was published in the autumn of 1949 and he wrote in reply to a letter of mine, on 13 November, 'It was written and rewritten under so many difficulties that I could not know what I had done. Yes, the Times is not very profound but I don't know if I want to be dissected yet—possibly my entrails will neither please the anatomists nor delight the simple reader. And I was surprised and grateful that anyone knew so much about the books, a good deal more than I know myself. I shall try to find out who it was. Meanwhile, of course, I have been wrestling with a new book for the last seven months and trying to keep it together in spite of changes of place and mood dependent on the family crisis.'

Trudy's illness was the family crisis in question. As I recall how total his devotion to her was and how deep his anxiety ever since April the year before, it seems to me all the more astonishing that he should have been able to bring off a novel of such exhilaration, verve, and pace as *A Fearful Joy* and then turn to a new novel so important to him as *A Prisoner of Grace*.

Trudy was by now ill beyond hope of recovery, hanging on to life out of sheer love of living and out of courage. Towards the end of November my own wife left for New Zealand, promising the children and Joyce and me that she would be back when the leaves returned to the trees and the blossom came out. I had preoccupations of my own in consequence and saw less of Joyce than I should. I did not realize Trudy's death was so close. She died on 13 December but it was two days before I knew. A friend, Margaret Taylor, rang to tell me. She had gone to Parks Road the day before with a sprig of heather for Trudy. 'She left yesterday,' Joyce said.

A few days later he rang me and asked me to supper in so natural a voice that I forgot Trudy was dead and so said nothing. Full of remorse I at once wrote him a note and when we met next evening we spoke of her, he calmer than I. She had prepared all the Christmas cards and ordered the tickets for the family visit to the pantomime—though not one for herself—so that the seasonal ritual so important for Joyce should not be broken. And so it happened. After the family gathering had dispersed, the festivities over, Joyce said, 'It was a good Christmas.'

In late March the leaves were beginning to show again and the blossom was on the flowering cherry and my wife returned. Joyce was now a lonely man, robbed of his emotional centre, hungry for the warmth of friendship and of family life. He began to drop in for tea with our children from time to time, sitting with one eye screwed up quizzically and listening to their sayings. He was delighted with the way one of my daughters in a meta-physical phase dealt with the darker side of eschatology. She refused to believe in hell. 'The bad angels couldn't have made it and the good angels wouldn't have. And God wouldn't have either, even though he could have, because he is good.'

The novels were now enjoying a great success in America and in Europe. Joyce was tempted to escape his loneliness and the familiar scenes of the grief he resolutely refused to show, and to seek out new countries and new people. He went to the United States in January 1951 and in the following summer he was off with some of his family to France. Later that year he was ill with something that was diagnosed as bursitis in the leg but appeared to pass off without leaving any traces. In the autumn of 1952 he was off again to Switzerland. In 1953 he was still restless and the death in February of his youngest son George, on the threshold of a brilliant scholarly career, was a severe blow, borne with the courage that by now we almost took for granted. In October he was writing to me from Washington: 'I am enjoying the whole journey, the friendly people, the busy towns, the rich countryside —just as I should enjoy a sleepy village on the moors, but with a different enjoyment. One needs a change. I shan't be back in Oxford until the tenth December—but I look forward very much to that time, and a large Christmas party again. I suppose Anna and Delia and Bridgy will have forgotten me when I come—but I rely upon your memory and Win's.'

On 15 November he wrote to my wife with a present for my daughter Brigid's birthday—he was a punctilious and generous observer of birthdays, especially those of children. 'The students here seem all gods—and I like young people, so keen and often so worried too. At Tulane I had seminars and talked to classes. I suppose I am an evangelist at bottom tho no church wd like my evangel. I long to see you all again, my dear, and love to Dan and

Anna, and Delia, and Bridgy and the garden and the canal, the cats and the fish.'

He was back in December, in plenty of time to prepare for the Christmas gathering when the house and its seven bedrooms would be full and ringing with the voices of his children and grandchildren. We had by now become part of his extended family and on Boxing Day we all went, with him as host, to the pantomime, taking up two rows. Afterwards we would go back to Parks Road, admire the Christmas tree, discuss the Christmas presents, watch the children play with their new toys, eat Christmas cake and mince pies, and drink tea or, for those with hangovers, something stronger. Nothing could induce him to be away at this time or at the New Year when we all gathered again to drink his special punch and at midnight open the windows to hear the whistles and sirens announce another year's beginning and pledge one another's health in champagne. For Joyce in those times each new year was always going to be, not just as good as the one before, but better.

These were the years, too, when he was wrestling with his political trilogy, learning to write without Trudy as his amanuensis, best critic, mistress of his thoughts and heart, and wife. The books did not come so easily as they had done before her death and the theme was obsessive for him, and complex in its working out. But when *A Prisoner of Grace* (1952), *Except the Lord* (1953), and *Not Honour More* (1955) had been published he was reasonably confident that he had done what he set out to do, expounded the politics of a nation and the politics of a family in terms of living characters. The Lord cannot build a house in politics, the message ran, without some interventions from the devil.

Every Wednesday he came to our house for tea, so as to enjoy the children's company, since by now our intimacy had established its own routines. He had become a kind of godfather to the children and he insisted on joining all birthday parties. I remember how often I came home from work at the end of the day to find him sitting happily in what I myself would have considered an intolerable clamour, missing nothing of the detail of their minute dramas and enjoying every shift in the kaleidoscope of childish emotions. In some of the short stories he wrote afterwards I can trace signs of the things he saw and heard among these children. And there is a passage in *Art and Reality* about a child's drawing of a swan which recalls a picture my daughter Delia drew for him of one of the swans from the canal at the bottom of our garden.

He had always told his own children stories when they were young, stories with recurring characters and wildly improbable adventures. Soon a ritual developed with us by which each time he came to tea he would tell our children and their friends an instalment of a serial that went on for years and, had it not been for illness and death and change, might have been going still for another generation. Each instalment ended in a fearful crisis from which it seemed impossible the hero or the heroine—always characters, however bizarre, with whom the listening children could identify—could ever escape. There he would halt and if the children pleaded with him to go on he would say he must go home or the soufflé his housekeeper was preparing for him would be ruined and she would be upset—an excuse I have heard him use to escape from other, less agreeable, occasions. Then, next Wednesday, he would be back and after tea the next instalment would begin with an ingenious solution that delivered hero or heroine and ended the children's suspense, only to work up again into another 'cliff-hanger'.

From these stories, ephemeral and alas unrecorded, one learned a lot about his writing; primitive in form as they were, working in wonder rather than probability and beautifully adapted to their purpose, they were true to the timeless principles of narrative, they showed the same prodigality and exuberance of invention, the movement and vigour, the power of empathy, the imaginative daring, that in the novels give back the sense of life in all its improbable profusion and vitality to the fiction of our time.

On Sundays he often came to lunch and afterwards we would go for a walk over Port Meadow and along the river to the Trout or through the Parks admiring the ducks. Sometimes a friend with a car took us further afield and Joyce was present at one of our own tragedies when Kate, our schnauzer bitch, climbed the tower of Rycote church behind us without our noticing and, in her eagerness to enjoy whatever we were enjoying, jumped on the parapet to see the view, and fell to the ground, mortally injured.

On Sunday evenings we gathered at Parks Road before dinner. The children would retire to the background (sometimes dressing up in the eighteenth-century dresses which Joyce had inherited and kept in his family hoard). The adults were in the conversational ascendant. All his intimate friends would try to be there, David and Rachel Cecil, Enid Starkie, Helen Gardner, Peter Ady, Audrey Beecham, Iris Murdoch, Wallace Robson, and stray friends from the outer world like Robert Lusty or William Empson, or Heneage Ogilvie.

He was the ideal host for people like these who were all in their various ways great talkers, for though loving to talk himself he was not a greedy talker. He was a skilful listener and gave his companions the feeling that they were talking well, and he was as warm and sympathetic in the tête-à-tête as he was unobtrusively able to orchestrate the larger groups. Indeed, he liked all the graces of living, though simple in himself, and was the best of hosts. Even when there were no guests, he always sat down to table with a certain formality behind which lay, not a formality of soul, but a feeling, something like a regular soldier's, that it was dangerous to relax too much, to let go: that traditions which had been built up, rituals which cemented family and society, should not be allowed lightly to dissolve. In this he resembled his own Mr. Wilcher of *To Be a Pilgrim*, rather than the artist prototype, Gulley Jimson. He knew that life was impossible without change but he knew also that life inconsistently hungered for an ultimately impossible stability.

Alone or not, he dined always, as long as he was able, in the family dining-room, surrounded by family portraits from the eighteenth and nineteenth centuries—for he was pious of family history, though not ostentatious—and the silver candlesticks threw a gleam on the plate and the mahogany and the decanter of fine claret as he moved meditatively through his correct succession of courses. Yet he ate and drank sparingly, being a notably temperate man. Nothing in him was out of control. He was a soldier not far

from his campaign, austere but without puritanism, often reminding me of Field Marshal Alexander, another Ulsterman whose
father had died young, in his calm and in his good manners, as
well as in the clarity of his eyes.

Cary was a man who thought and felt deeply on every subject.
In politics he was definitely not a man of either right or left,
though what he believed he believed with passion. He voted
Liberal whenever he could and was a member of that party. But
he was empirical. The way to get a thing done and whether it
could be done modified his opinion of what ought to be done. On
the question of censorship he was absolutely committed to freedom, what would nowadays be called permissive, vehemently so,
in fact.

There were times when he seemed to speak as an Irishman but,
after Ireland became a republic and perhaps before, he considered
himself an Englishman whose family had happened to live in
Ireland for three hundred years. He was very pro-English in the
best sense. This sometimes made him seem inconsistent. He had
been violently anti-Munich in 1938, because he thought that it
was bad for what was best in England, in this case shorthand for
what was best in the world. Yet he was not anti-Suez, a point of
disagreement with us. But we had to forgive him, because from
his point of view Suez made a sort of sense: his misgivings were
that it might fail, not that it was, as we passionately felt, wrong.

At the base of his love of England was the political freedom so
deeply rooted there. For him, intellectually, freedom was the
most important thing of all and injustice part of the price we have
to pay for it. But almost as important as freedom was the need to
do only what was expedient at a given moment. He did not
believe that the end justified the means but that the end was itself
shaped by the means.

His conversation was not necessarily literary, for the range of
his interests was very wide and so was his experience. With me
and others like me who had some knowledge of war he delighted
to talk of battles, of courage and of fear and of men's behaviour
under strain. He loved spell-binders and rogues and loved to hear
anecdotes about eccentrics, confidence tricksters, politicians,

adventurers, or stories about what children, those other beings capable of being themselves without self-consciousness, said and did, or high academic gossip with its low tricks, or tales from the outer political world. For sometimes he fretted at the narrowness of Oxford. It was 'a hotbed of cold feet', he once said to a friend. And after Trudy's death he liked to talk of the world of his young manhood, the world before 1914, and how beautiful its beautiful women were.

With critics like Helen Gardner or David Cecil the conversation was always likely to take a literary turn, if only because literature was an endless resource of examples. Joyce's admirations among novelists were few and firm and unaffected by fashion. The great European novelists of the nineteenth century were those he read and re-read, though he would sometimes say that Conrad was the only novelist who had influenced him. No writer's work, even the work of those he admired, was immune from his criticism but the criticism was stimulating because it was made from the point of view of a fellow novelist, not that of a critic looking from the outside.

I think I valued his talk most when he was discussing the craft of writing as he knew it in his own work—if only I could remember more of what he said. I do remember his advice that you should always draw for yourself the plan and elevation of the house in which your characters lived; not that I have followed it. And how he used to say that if your novel was likely to be held up by a long but inescapable piece of dialogue you should get the characters into a train or a taxi, so that the reader would be given the illusion of movement even though the narrative itself was not in motion. Another stratagem he recommended concerned over-mighty minor characters who threatened to usurp too big a place in a novel. The thing to do, if you could not get rid of them altogether, was to diminish them by taking away their names.

In 1953 I was warned that I ought to have a gall-bladder operation and was advised to get my weight down by a stone or two beforehand. I took up squash, as the only violent exercise for which I had time, and by early March next year was sufficiently lean for surgery. Joyce mentioned my case to Heneage Ogilvie.

Heneage, as I now see Joyce probably intended, insisted on carrying out the operation himself, without fee and making the necessary arrangements at Guy's Hospital. While I was there Joyce sent
me a copy of Dostoevsky's wife's diary. 'I should miss you a great
deal if you did not return to these parts . . . I have always thought
this book a masterpiece, both for the picture of D. and even more,
the unconscious revelation of the girl, Anna.'

The main work on *Not Honour More* was still far from over but
Joyce himself was in need of a holiday. In March 1954 he went
off to Italy and the south of France with his sister-in-law, Mary
Ogilvie, and was reminded again of Dostoevsky. 'Mary and I
wandered over to Monaco yesterday, studied queer fish in the
museum and strange humanity at the tables, lost a little money at
the tables and bussed home. We are thoroughly lazy but I have
had some first-class thoughts about the book and I am looking
forward to my next work on it.'

In June he had a visit from John and Mary Middleton Murry.
Murry and Joyce had long been estranged and had not met since
John was not at home to Joyce in 1912, but lately Murry had
written out of the blue and said that he now realized that it was
Joyce and not himself who had turned out to be the genius. No
doubt this was an embarrassing thing for Joyce to deal with—
Murry was always most embarrassing when he was being most
scrupulous—but a visit to Oxford was arranged and Joyce gave a
dinner party for the Murrys with Mary Ogilvie, the Cecils, and
ourselves as supporting guests.

I had meant to ask Murry something about Katherine Mansfield but he looked to me so worn and scarred by life that I
relented, thinking how often any questions I might ask must have
been asked already and how tiresome it must be to be constantly
interrogated about a phase of your life that was thirty and more
years behind you and about someone who, however much you
valued her at the time, you had not quite expected to be so much
more interesting, dead and in retrospect, than your living, surviving, so much maturer and wiser self.

The evening went off agreeably and the Murrys themselves
were charming; but it was clear enough to Joyce and Murry and

the rest of us that too much time and separate experience had divided them for too long and that the old warm friendship of their youth could no more be revived than youth itself. Time does not allow these things to return. And Joyce himself was tired, though the ravage showed less on him than on Murry. Perhaps Joyce was more than just tired. Enid Starkie saw him in Paris later that year and thought that he looked weary and that he seemed to be dragging one foot a little.

Not Honour More gave him a good deal of trouble. Because it was the last volume of his political trilogy it was important for the other two volumes and for the whole trilogy as well as important in itself. And for Jim Latter he was drawing, one surmises, a little on his own younger African self. While he was so deeply living in that character we noticed that his own everyday language took a coarser, more colloquial turn and four-letter words began to bob up in his vocabulary, something never noticeable in his speech before and vanishing from it again not long after the novel was finished. I have noticed something of the same sort happen when old soldiers meet and suddenly find themselves using a language that they have not used since they left the army. It was particularly striking at this time in Joyce, however, because he had never practised the freedom of language so characteristic of the 'emancipated' artists of our time.

Indeed, something of Jim Latter's impulsive restlessness seemed to invade his whole behaviour that year. In June and July he was off again, to West Germany and Berlin, on lecture tours; in October he was in Paris; and in November and December he was in Sweden, Finland, and Denmark.

A letter to me from Helsinki dated 5 December opens in a way that did not seem like the Joyce we had known. For he described himself as lying in bed in his hotel, waiting for breakfast. 'I always wait to be taken—it is the only way to conserve energy. Upsala nearly killed me—with sight-seeing.' He found the Finns a lively and exciting people, perhaps because they were only 25 kilometres from the Russian frontier—but then I cannot recall a people whom he had not found lively and exciting. Less expected were his complaints about the remorseless sightseeing and then, at the end of the day, being put on a platform 'to talk to 400 people with rather sketchy English about the diseases of the symbol'.

But he soon laughed himself out of the querulous strain with a description of a dinner in Stockholm to which his Swedish publisher had invited all the prominent critics. The meal over, the publisher read aloud the reviews the critics had written of the first of Joyce's novels to be translated into Swedish. 'This was embarrassing for us all—the expressions of some of the critics as they saw their turn coming and tried to remember how rude they had been—the cautious glances at me to see how I was taking it all—were pure film, by Orson Welles.'

The sacred ceremonies of Christmas and New Year drew him back to Oxford but did not hold him for long. On 16 January 1955 he was off again, this time to lecture in Greece. The start was unpromising: an accident in a foggy take-off shook everyone badly but he boarded the next aircraft. Within the week he was writing from Athens. Delphi was 'unexpected in its completeness and its character. I hadn't expected all the ex-voto temples shelving their spoils taken from each other. What a contentious people they were even then.' The Acropolis was magnificent in the massiveness of its pillars but the Theseum was 'too perfect, too much the acme of good taste—of refinement. I don't mind refinement but I like it dynamic. The other kind is too smug.'

This was to be his last visit abroad, though he did not then know it. On his return he did not feel well and saw his doctor. Something was seriously wrong with his leg now but various consultations throughout the spring and summer of 1955 produced no firm diagnosis or effective treatment. Not till November was there a certain verdict: he had amyotrophic lateral sclerosis. He would steadily lose the use of his limbs and eventually the paralysis would extend to the rest of his body. At most he could live for four or five years. A span of two years or less was more probable.

He had already, after his return from Greece, buckled down at last to what he meant to be a religious trilogy, 'The Captive and the Free', a work he had been brooding over for years and which he intended to contain, expressed through characters and action, his maturest views about religion, the summa of his whole belief as an artist and a man. It had often come up in his conversation as his most cherished and difficult project, something that was to be the capstone of his work. The title itself gnomically summed up his view of the condition of man; captive because of his physiology, his mortality, his need of others; in so far as he possessed imagination, the power to create his own life, transcend the conditions of his captivity, free. Some are wholly captive, I used to think as I listened to Joyce expound his theme, and none are wholly free. Joyce himself at that time seemed to be the nearest you could get to freedom.

By August 1955 he was deeply engaged. He wrote to me on 8 August in the Scillies where I was on a working holiday. 'I too am having a holiday as the new novel has laid hold of me and carried me off to a new world of feeling and among a lot of new people. It is exciting to get to know them. How baffling one's own characters are before one penetrates through their small talk to the springs of thought and nature.'

On the first page of *The Horse's Mouth* Gulley Jimson says: 'And I perceived that I hadn't time to waste on pleasure. A man of my age has to get on with the job.' This was now Joyce's situation. In December 1955, he would be sixty-seven. And his disability threatened to close on him very fast. The novel clamoured to be written. 'I shall die if I don't finish this book,' he said to my wife, and there was grimness in the jest. Fortunately he acquired at last that autumn a really good secretary, Edith Millen, who had been trained as a nurse; and a devoted housekeeper, Mrs. Lightburne. For now he had taken stock of his remaining time and strength and reorganized his life, like a commander preparing for a long series of withdrawals under enemy pressure.

He ceased working in the top attic as the stairs became impossible for him and began to use Trudy's old private sitting-room on the ground floor as his study. He had metal grips fitted into the walls of the passages at various strategic points and with their aid and that of a stick could for a time get about without other help. When the disease attacked his hands he contrived a sling with an elastic band which could take the weight of his wrist and leave him free to write.

Absorbed though he was in the novel he could not altogether resist some exciting distractions. Norman Rosten had consulted him about a dramatized version of *Mr. Johnson* and Joyce, when he read the script, was full of suggestions. We were amused: for Joyce was only able to criticize another man's work—novel or play or film—in terms of what he himself would have done. If it did not interest him at all it was dismissed as a 'bit of stuff'. If it did engage him, then he would exclaim aloud at the author's failure to see his own essential theme or to find the right technique for it. So that to go to a play or a film with him was not so much to see the thing for itself as to be involved in a different version which Joyce would be creating as it went along. He lacked that power of surrender which enables a man to be a passive spectator, a captive audience.

He was also working that year, 1955, on the Clark Lectures for Cambridge University in which he hoped to bring together— did eventually bring together—and expound in theoretical form the views about art and life which he had so stubbornly pondered for so many years and which his novels presented in fictional form. And as time went on, no longer stretching infinitely in front of him, these lectures became for him another summa, parallel with and eventually competing for time with 'The Captive and the Free'.

And then there were the illustrations he was supposed to do for a special edition printed on Herbert Davis's hand press at Bodley of 'The Old Strife at Plant's'. This was a chapter which had been written for *The Horse's Mouth* but which Joyce had excluded from the final version of the novel because it was in some way disproportionate. It had been a particular favourite of Trudy's and she had preserved it from destruction. Now he was drawing, his hand supported by the sling, sketches of Gulley in pursuit of his Pink, and chuckling fondly as he recalled the time of the original writing and memories of Trudy came vividly back to him. When the time came for the colours to be filled in, however, he could not manage them and this was done, under his careful supervision, by Herbert Davis's daughter and my daughter Anna. The sketches of Gulley have a certain look of Gerald Wilde about them, and of Dylan Thomas.

There was also the special limited edition of *The Horse's Mouth* to be published by Rainbird. For this he was able to do only a self-portrait, a head, drawing it direct on to the zinc plate with almost the last strength of his hand. It is a superb likeness of a suffering, wise, and courageous man; the head of a man alert to confront his last, indeed his only, enemy. When one of my daughters said to him, 'It's very like you, Joycie, but why do you look so grim?' he answered gaily, 'It's because I was looking in a mirror, my dear.' He was indeed looking in a mirror and saw plainly but with courage the death in his own face. And it was about this time that my wife said to him, 'I do think you are behaving very bravely about all this, Joyce.' 'I don't think it's really brave,' he said. 'There are situations where there is only one thing to do. And this is one of them. I have no choice.'

The time came when he had to take to a wheel-chair. In fact he had been using one at intervals since the earlier months of the year for longer excursions. But he could not always be persuaded to go out in it. Once in the spring my wife said to him, 'It's a lovely spring day, Joyce. Let me take you to the Parks.' But he shook his head. 'I have sixty springs in my head.'

His last excursion was to St. Giles' Fair in September. It had always been his practice to take our children. For he loved fairs, and how often they occur in his novels. On one occasion he had sent the children into the Flea Circus while he stood outside in his old macintosh and cloth cap holding their balloons. He was much diverted, and a little mortified, to find himself mistaken by passers-by for a balloon seller. This last time, he insisted on going on the Big Wheel, sitting between my two younger daughters. Although he was barely able to totter from the wheel-chair to his seat, once the Wheel began to turn he was full of gaiety, laughing, eyes shining, waving to my wife and turning to each of the girls in turn, to enjoy their enjoyment.

There was one more serious interruption to his work on the novel and the Clark Lectures, a stay in Stoke Mandeville Hospital where treatment with a new drug administered by intravenous drip seemed worth trying. We visited him whenever we could and always found him cheerful, absorbed in the life of the hospital and ceaselessly thinking about his work, rallying the company, prepared to entertain hopes of a cure, even if only to encourage his friends, but fundamentally expecting nothing.

On 27 November 1956 he wrote to my daughter. 'My darling Brigid. How well you write. When my mail came in, on my breakfast tray, I looked at all the writings and said: Who's *this* from Oxford—which professor—and I was terrifically astonished to see that it was from you. I'm writing my best now but I can't write so well as you and usually my writing is quite atrocious— poor Miss Millen has a fearful struggle to make out my M.S.S.'

The treatment failed and he came home again. His speech was slurred now and his light voice lighter. It was not difficult for him to chart the enemy's progress. He could feel a 'flicker' in the nerve of each muscle as it was attacked and the paralysis edged its way forward. That flicker continued night and day, as sleepless as time. One by one the muscles of his limbs were defeated and with the defeat of each outpost, he was deprived of one more capacity. The time came when he could not get in or out of bed or take a bath without help. A canvas sling on a metal crane was designed by John Payne, a friend of Audrey Beecham's, to overcome the difficulty and he wrote to Brigid—we were staying at Barmoor Castle in Northumberland where he had once spent a summer holiday with us—and told her how successful the crane was and how Edith could now put him to bed with its aid.

Through all these months he had still insisted on the children's coming to tea and for their serial and he was happy also in having his grandson Lucius with him at week-ends; for Lucius was now at the Dragon School where Joyce's sons had been, a continuity that gave Joyce much pleasure.

We and all his friends were in and out of the house very much in those days and there were visitors from all over the world—not only journalists and interviewers but many of the old friends and new friends also. It was about this time that we brought our American friends James and Marie-Louise Osborn to see him; a visit that so impressed them that, after his death, they bought his manuscript archive and presented it to Bodley. It was no strain to visit him: one was never conscious of reluctantly complying with the appropriate beatitude in coming to his bedside; for his courage did not embarrass but made one think better of the human race for having been able to produce such a man. And he did not repine for the lost future or the lost past. Gratitude in most people is the most grudging of the emotions but in him it welled up, for a happy life, for Trudy, for his children, for his friends, and was untainted by regret for what had been given and taken away.

One could not fail to read the physical signs, however brightly the old spirit still burnt in the dying lamp. My diary for 13 October 1956 reads: 'He can scarcely use a pen at all now. Dictates, but the voice is beginning to go. A desperate, slow tragedy. The development of this will overcast our whole winter and I fear he cannot live much beyond that.'

He was not well enough, of course, to deliver the first of the Clark Lectures on 19 October or to go and hear his nephew Robert Ogilvie do it for him. Earlier in the month he had written to me in the Scillies and complained of the time they were costing him. 'It is very frustrating to have to break off my novel over and over again for these odd jobs, but, thank goodness, the thing is nearly done now.' And, even if he was not well enough for the lecture, he was sufficiently consoled by the reports of friends who were able to get to Cambridge. My diary notes about this time that he was 'very frail but more cheerful and working on his novel again'. And on one particularly successful day he said to my wife, 'The novel's in the bag.'

He was in bed all the time now and working under heartbreakingly difficult conditions. He now had a bed-desk invented by himself and made for him by his next-door neighbour, a magistrate whom Joyce called 'the Judge'. A roll of blank paper ran underneath and led across the desk to another spool on which the used paper was wound. At first, he still had enough movement in his right hand to be able to push the paper forward as it was used. When this, too, became impossible his son Tristram devised an electrical switch by which Joyce dropped his wrist on a button and the paper moved forward automatically. The hand itself was supported by a sling and the pen or pencil was fastened to the fingers. I used to marvel that a man so close to death did not despair of art, that he could still keep at bay that sense of 'nada' which overcomes so many writers even when death is still distant.

Though his voice was now little better than a whisper and had to be jealously husbanded he was still adamant that his friends should gather every Sunday night as of old and have drinks and talk. To him 'laughter in the next room' was not something to make him feel cut off and repine but an affirmation that life went on and would go on after him. And one by one they would come in and talk to him for a little. We all tried to store up tales and anecdotes that would amuse him—indeed to this day his friends will occasionally say of something, some incident or scene, 'that would have amused Joyce'. By far the most successful was David Cecil, the man with whom he had always liked talking most, and who was now able to disguise better than any of us the grief he felt for Joyce and find a steady stream of interesting and amusing talk that left it unnecessary for Joyce himself to strain his resources by trying to whisper a bridge across silences.

We all feared by now that he would not live till Christmas, the one that was bound to be his last. But we underrated his stubborn spirit and the force over him that was exercised by a family occasion to which he could look forward. Part of his abundant life had been his power to enjoy all of it—the past which enriched the quieter reveries of the present and which in his case seemed to be unburdened by guilt and self-reproach or any sense of failure; and the future which was always immunized for him by hope and which even now could still offer joy if by an effort of will he contracted hope to the shorter views Sydney Smith long ago recommended, views that enabled him to see and feel the family round him at least once more. So Christmas and the family came and the New Year; and his presence in the adjoining room, though we were all filled with sorrow and foreboding, still radiated courage and cheerfulness and made the ritual celebrations a success against the odds, something not macabre.

Once only did he break down. On Christmas Eve, his grandson

Lucius, at Joyce's request, sang 'O Little Town of Bethlehem'. The doorway of the bedroom was open so that Lucius, standing in the doorway, could hear the piano. When it was over, Joyce burst into tears. The injustice of life and the knowledge of what he was losing overcame him.

By January he knew he would not live long enough to carry through the task of revising and 'jointing up' the novel—which he had long since decided must be compressed into a single volume, not three—and also revise the Clark Lectures for publication, a task which he regarded as a duty. He accepted that he would not finish 'The Captive and the Free' and would indeed die. Even so, he would not give in but, having finished the Clark Lectures, began to write short stories, things he knew he could finish because they were short. It was typical of him that these last stories should be full of an ironical gaiety.

In the middle of March he finished polishing his last short story. Thereafter even he could write no longer and he and we were waiting for the end. He died on 29 March 1957.

Joyce would have smiled sadly to himself, thinking of Mr. Wilcher and the Adams salon in Tolbrook Manor and its fate, if he could have seen what was to happen to the house in Parks Road, still standing but converted to a scientific annexe and dominated and overlooked by huge new scientific buildings. And his friends cannot pass it without remembering his courage and generosity and the eagerness with which he recognized such ironies of change even while he grieved over them. For he accepted that change was the stuff of life, its condition, and that grief is the price of happiness just as the last change is the price of living.

A Spinning Man

Dylan Thomas

6

A Spinning Man

DYLAN THOMAS
(1914-1953)

> . . . as I hack
> This rumpus of shapes
> For you to know
> How I, a spinning man,
> Glory also this star, bird
> Roared, sea born, man torn, blood best.
>
> DYLAN THOMAS

IN the last twelve months of the war, if the Fitzrovia–Soho circuit was one of your routines as it was one of mine, Dylan Thomas was a difficult man not to know; it took longer to find out that he was impossible to know, or at least more than one of him at a time, and that one only for a time. He was working on scripts for Donald Taylor of Gryphon Films in those days and, though he spent as much of his time as he could renewing himself in his beloved Wales, he was a good deal in London and often to be seen or found in the Wheatsheaf or the Marquis of Granby or the Fitzroy.

At first I barely knew him to speak to and was diffident, partly because of my admiration for his poetry and partly because of its growing fame, about pressing to a closer acquaintance. In any case it would not have been easy. I was still a major in the New Zealand army and this was not an advantage among people who had not fought in the war: one was defensive about the aggressions that might arise from putting them on the defensive. Moreover, I was a friend of Julian Maclaren-Ross and this was a serious

obstacle. For, though Julian and Dylan had both worked for
Donald Taylor and had got on well together, they were wary of
each other. Julian was a conversational monopolist and exacted
total attention from his audience—something Dylan, himself
always his own centre and never short of listeners though much
better than Julian at listening, would never have been willing to
concede. Besides, they both had the power or the weakness of
always spending immediately any money that came to them, and
were therefore constantly in need of admirers with money to lend.
And, like rival *condottieri*, they preferred to command their own
sources, if not their own resources, each carrying with him an
invisible but perceptible social territory into which the other did
not intrude. So, when Dylan came into the Wheatsheaf, he always
turned right at the door; Julian, who never seemed to arrive in
the Wheatsheaf but always to be already there, kept his station
and standing at the corner of the bar on the left. And, when bitter
ran out at the Wheatsheaf (the pubs were rationed and thirst
exceeded supply) and it was necessary to cross to the Marquis,
Julian, after a friendly salute to Dylan who might be with Augustus John and Nina Hamnett and sometimes his wife, Caitlin,
would proceed to a distant table with his own court.

All this, though the restraints on mingling were somewhat vex-
ing, on the whole amused me, interested as I have always been by
the social devices the British in their crowded cities and island
have evolved for mutual sufferance and survival. But I had a further restraint of my own to contend with; for reading Dylan's
poetry before and during the war had made me decide, in the
face of baffled recognition of its power, that I must abandon my
own poetic ambitions. If his subtleties of sound and rhythm and
technique and that dense obscurity which seemed so penetrable to
his other admirers were to be the standard, then I must reconcile
myself to licking my wounds in prose. So that it was appropriate
that I should find myself confined to the company, exclusive and
excluding, of Julian, a writer of stories, a man of prose.

Even so, I was soon to find that this simple distinction would
not do. Some time in 1945, when I was laid up with flu, my wife
brought me from the library Dylan's *Portrait of the Artist as a*

Young Dog. I read it with greed and admiration and had to acknowledge to myself that Dylan had also, if he wished, the
makings of a master in prose. Only the title seemed unworthy,
a facetious fleer at James Joyce.

Not long after, one Saturday morning, I was alone in the
Wheatsheaf, Julian being away staying with friends in Bognor.
Dylan came in and we joined each other over a pint of bitter. I
told him I had been reading his stories and how much I admired
them. I had myself written stories about childhood and youth in
New Zealand and we talked easily of our vernal pasts and the
problems of making them the stuff of art, making the provincial
setting of the young individual into something that was universal.
In the end, impertinently I suppose but in genuine perplexity, I
asked him why he had parodied Joyce's title. His brown eyes
bulged at me and then down to his beer, dog-hung. He explained
that he hadn't read James Joyce at the time.

I was startled, shocked. I could not see how he could have
written the stories without having read Joyce. My judgement was
very much at fault if behind them there wasn't at least the influence of *Dubliners*. But it was my habit, then as now, to try to
believe what people said when there seemed no obvious reason
why they shouldn't be telling the truth; in those days perhaps
more out of naïveté, and nowadays because I feel that other
people's lies are a form of truth. It was not till long afterwards
that I learnt Dylan had indeed read Joyce, and carefully, and that
even before his book was published friends had questioned the
title he proposed and got little satisfaction for answer. But by the
time I learnt this I already knew from much listening to Dylan
that he was from time to time overcome by a strange compulsion
to give evasive answers to simple questions, invent unnecessary
falsehoods, construct complicated fantasies, as if there were something too boring about the simple truth, or as if the muscles of his
imagination occasionally insisted on flexing themselves however
inappropriate the occasion.

Shortly after this an American friend of ours from pre-war days
turned up to stay. He had been a prisoner of war in Colditz and
was famished for the renewal of life. One Saturday evening we

took him to the Wheatsheaf with us. Dylan was there and others whom we knew, though not Julian. The evening prospered and when the pubs closed we all took bottles, at the invitation of a friend named Lucile, to her flat in Riding House Street. All I remember now of the party that followed is the superb voice of Dylan as he recited for us some rather bawdy songs and verses he had lately been writing, things he seemed to regard as written for fun rather than in earnest. They were a sort of *vers de société*, except that the society was Welsh and humble, people from a village which Dylan said was called Laugharne but which in the verses he had named Llareggub. The verses, quatrains for the most part, were rich in affection, humour, compassion, and vivifying detail, and their effect was somehow medieval in the intimacy of the alliance between the poet and the people he was describing— an unsought touch of Chaucer or even of Langland. I had had much too much to drink and I remember my admiration and enjoyment being infiltrated and spoilt by a feeling of dismal envy for the remarkable flow of metaphor and fantasy which came so easily to the man—came from him, rather, as water pours from a fountain. I left the room of the party and stood glumly drunk at the window on a landing of the stair, until my wife and our American friend collected me and we went home to Notting Hill Gate. It was a chastening experience for me to feel such jealousy and, I now think, an important part of my growing up.

In the autumn of that year, 1945, I left the army and went to Oxford to work and live. I had been tempted to become a writer by profession and had decided instead to work in an office for my living.

When, early in 1946, Dylan's *Deaths and Entrances* was published, I hastened to buy a copy. In format it was rather a mean little book—the war was over but still imposed its economies— and I remember feeling puzzled and irritated over what then seemed to me the precious ingenuity by which the first part of the poem 'Vision and Prayer' was written and set up in lines that shaped a diamond on six successive pages while the second part was a chalice or hour-glass on the corresponding six. I doubt if I discerned, or would have felt sympathy for, the undertones of a Nativity poem and what would have seemed to me a regression to a Christian motif. And I had forgotten George Herbert's poem 'Easter Wings'. But I liked the poems better than any of his I had read hitherto and, better still for a plain man, found them more intelligible.

It didn't occur to me, I think, to write to him about the book and I probably wouldn't have done so if it had. It is never easy to write such letters and Dylan didn't strike me as a man who would particularly welcome them. Poetry for him, I had the impression, was a serious matter, no more to be talked about than one's love for one's wife. The situation where such talk might be possible would have to be very special, one of much greater intimacy and confidence than existed between us.

When I bought the book I did not know that Dylan had just about then come to live in Oxford, in a tiny cottage in Holywell Ford belonging to Alan and Margaret Taylor, old friends of his but not at this time known to me. I worked every night at that period on my own writing and allowed myself only a Saturday lunch-time venture into the bookshops and the pubs. It was not until the middle of September that we ran into each other in the Cornmarket. I knew that the Gloucester Arms had bitter—you had to keep well informed and move from one pub to another if you were not to be reduced to a vile dark oily brew called Burton —and so we went there. The meeting was important to me, hungry as I was for literary company and especially such company as his; of sufficient importance for me to note it in my diary and hope for its recurrence.

We talked, it seems, about sexual potency and sexual promiscuity, among other things, but my note doesn't make it clear which of us contended that promiscuity was a kind of Damaroid —a patent promoter of male vigour familiar in the shop windows of Charing Cross Road. We agreed that constancy was the real thing, so I guess we must have been praising marriage and our wives. I was writing at that time a story called 'Not Substantial Things' which is set in wartime Italy and which ends with the narrator awaking with a hangover and reflecting that truth is what you think and feel when you have a hangover; that health and well-being can be enjoyed only at the expense of truth, illusion being their necessary condition. It was a theory which Dylan had the experience to understand.

He must have talked also about his own circumstances, the problem of being a poet, and therefore broke, and yet being married and a father. For, the following week, I discussed his case with the then Secretary of the Oxford University Press, Kenneth Sisam, and whether there was anything we could do. Sisam thought something might be done through the Rockefeller Foundation which had enabled us to help many refugee scholars during the war but nothing ever came of this and I cannot now recall how far we pursued it.

Dylan and I met again from time to time during the rest of the year, usually on a Saturday morning after I had left the office. Dylan was leading a fairly hand-to-mouth sort of life, getting what money he got from work on films, the occasional fee for a poem or a broadcast, windfalls of various kinds. It was a precarious existence: he had to be in London often, drifting round pubs and friends in order to keep up the necessary contacts and because he was in any case gregarious, casual, improvident, not given to carefully planned courses of action though full of fantasies of planning. Money got this way was fairy gold, spent in its own getting. Trying to bring it back to Oxford was like trying to carry beef tea in a colander.

There was nothing I could do to help, and I was only partly aware of how desperate his situation often was. In any case, my own salary was very small and, though I had chosen a regular job deliberately to avoid the life he was having to lead, I had little enough to come and go on. And it seemed to me then, indeed to some extent it really was so, that Dylan was always going to fall on his feet: his genius was so obvious, his charm so compelling and his nature so lovable, that he would always find friends or patrons. And I did not realize that behind the fecklessness there was a pride, none the less fierce for being intermittent or stifled by desperation, and that there was in Dylan also a man who longed for independence, though incapable of the steady application to things that would make money or of economies that would at least prevent him from spending what he had.

Anyhow, whenever we met, he at least had enough for drinks, and for the cigarettes that were always drooping wetly from his red lower lip. Given a pint in his hand and a cigarette in his mouth he could quickly pass from a state of gloom, if only by immoderately describing and outrageously exaggerating whatever had occasioned it, to a buoyancy, a plateau of comedy and good humour, where he was purged for the moment of his worries and where you, as if you were in a theatre where he was the player, were also free of the harassing quotidian. And it was this gift, the art of imparting freedom from the care of life and yet making life seem fuller and fairer, that drew people to him. 'He's as good as a play', my own parents would have said of him, had they known him. And we too seldom reflected that he paid for the tickets, not us.

On the whole he preferred, as I did myself, to avoid the more intellectually ambitious kinds of conversation, anything overtly literary or about art or anything theorizing or abstract. Talk in a pub was, after all, an escape from the office or the study, the places where in solitude one wrestled with what was difficult. Much better to revel in amused gossip about one's friends or exaggerated anecdotes about their or one's own more ludicrous predicaments. Thus I recall one long tale of his from this time which recounted how in a night club he had been crazy enough to hit a waiter. The next thing he remembered was coming to on the floor realizing that he had a sprained ankle and that several hard steely little men were bashing away at him like pneumatic drills. And the manager saying: 'What! A fucking cripple! Here, get out of the way and let me have a go at him.'

And he had another long, very Welsh story about a postman who, taken short in a ditch while going his country rounds, had caught his testicles in a rabbit trap. Having been brought up in the New Zealand countryside, and indeed caught more than once in a rabbit trap myself though by nothing more vital than the fingers, I enjoyed this side of his repertory. It reminded me of many not dissimilar tales told by the immigrant Irish of New Zealand: tales which made the hard life of the land, lived close to the cows and the horses and the pigs and the dogs, just that much easier to bear; product of the endless art which transmutes the tedium of the day into comedy by the hearth at night.

The fact that I had been a Catholic seemed at times to have a fearful fascination for him, or for the latent Welsh nonconformist in him; but I think he also realized that whatever the form of the Christianity in a Celtic countryside—Welsh or Irish—it has a primitiveness in common, a kind of provincial puritanism. We were alike, also, in that we had each lost his father's language. And I noticed that, however he might talk of women, it was the way the young men I had known had talked, with little reference to actual women, and with more bravado than real salacity, a kind of boyish delight in being a man among men that Dylan never quite grew out of.

His wife, Caitlin, I did not at that time know, except what might be inferred from Dylan's obvious devotion to her and occasional gossip I had heard about her beauty and strangeness of temper. Once, when Dylan had come home to lunch with me after the pub, to the delight of my wife and daughters, we made an arrangement by which he and Caitlin and their two children were to come to tea the next day, Sunday. But Caitlin rang after lunch and said Dylan had passed out; which seemed likely enough, though I was left with a tiny suspicion that she might not be willing to meet any more of Dylan's pub friends.

By this time, in Third Programme circles at least, Dylan was making his name as a broadcaster. After I had listened to him in a production of David Jones's *In Parenthesis* my diary became enthusiastic. 'A rich voice, stirring the mesh of nerves that only the best can reach.' I went to look for him the next morning in the Turf, at this period his favourite pub, though whether I found him or not I can't now remember. I do recall that Reggie Smith came to Oxford around that time to arrange for a broadcast about Oxford in which both Dylan and I took part. There was a lunch beforehand at the Randolph in which we ate whale steaks and I could see behind Dylan's thanks to his host the same resolution as mine: that, whatever the rigours of rationing, we would never eat whale steak again.

It was about then that Dylan told me a burlesque story of meeting Henry Miller in London. After a prolonged session in the pubs they went to a little dairy in Rathbone Place which served sandwiches and which I well remember as being a very simple, clean, unpretentious place. But Miller was drunk and also extremely short-sighted. He was convinced that Dylan had taken him to a brothel and that the plain uniforms and innocent bearing of the waitresses were the last word in lubricious sophistication. Dylan had great difficulty in averting calamity and never succeeded at all in convincing Miller that he was mistaken. We speculated on how many similar misunderstandings might underlie the exploits so boringly recounted in *Tropic of Capricorn* and Dylan went on to improvise a new work of Miller's of which the dairy was the transmuted centre and in which Miller played a grotesquely comical role, rather like Mr. Magoo.

By the spring of 1947 the refuge in Holywell Ford had become for one reason or another impossible. Dylan must have been a tumultuary guest. And it would have been difficult for Caitlin, confined by children to the cottage and being a very proud person who always suspected that other people's generosity imposes obligations, and implies claims. She always had at heart the realization that nothing of their hard life made sense if it did not result in poetry; whereas, shuttling to and from between Oxford and London, spending time in the making of money and spending the money itself in wasting time, Dylan was not writing poetry. Friends managed to solve the situation temporarily by arranging for Dylan to get an Authors' Society grant; and the next time I ran into him he was just off to Italy with his family, full of expectations of happiness and time to write. I was reminded of the readiness with which D. H. Lawrence and Katherine Mansfield always believed that a change of place would solve their problems but repressed my fears that Dylan was bound to meet the disillusionment that always overtook them.

Sure enough, when I next met him in Oxford towards the end of 1947, he was fed up with Italy and glad to be back. His arm was in a sling but that was London's fault: trying to climb into his friend Bill McAlpine's house he had fallen and broken his arm—

he was accident-prone and his bones were very frangible. We drank cheerfully at the Gloucester Arms and he regaled me with stories of his Italian misadventures. When we parted he was off back to South Leigh near Witney where Margaret Taylor had bought a house for him and his family to live in.

Meanwhile Dylan still had to be constantly in London to make money by broadcasting or writing for films. Since he often missed his return train he would sometimes have to come home by hired car and, even though that might cost less than staying on in London and spending the money in pubs, it was not a way of living that helped keep the family going; and it did not entail the consolation which would enable Caitlin to endure any amount of poverty and privation: independence and the steady writing of poetry.

As Dylan's London circuit was now that of the BBC pubs and my occasional business in London did not lie that way and as he was less often in Oxford itself, I saw rather less of him in this period than formerly, apart from an occasional glimpse at the Perch in Binsey where we sometimes went on Sunday mornings with our children and he and Caitlin with theirs. But by now I was involved in the long-drawn-out fiasco of 'The Character of Ireland', which Louis MacNeice and Bertie Rodgers were to have edited, and from 1949 onwards this took me to London and into the BBC pubs which they used for both business and relaxation. And so I began to see more of Dylan among his London friends, though here it was much more difficult to have the comparatively intimate conversation that had been possible in the pubs of Oxford. I liked his old friends, people like John Davenport—if there ever was anyone quite like John Davenport—but Dylan was usually accompanied by a crowd of hangers-on, like a bull in a field surrounded by flies, and was too good-natured to rid himself of them.

Another difficulty was that I could not drink as much as formerly; my life was now much more tied to routines and appointments and business, and I was not free as the others were to follow the moment's impulse, spend the afternoons in the ML Club or the Mandrake, come back to the Stag or the George or the Dover

Castle at opening time in the evening and then go on to whatever party might be going. My trains had to be caught, my appearances next morning in my office, punctual and compos, were absolutely necessary.

It was through 'The Character of Ireland' that Dylan first came to spend the night in our house, after an epic evening in the George in Oxford, when I have never seen him more brilliant in his wit and fantasy. I did not get to bed till four that morning and, when the children had left for school and I set off for the office at nine, the house was silent. Later, my wife recalls, there were thunderous groans and bursts of coughing upstairs, as if some asthmatic titan in the attic were coming to doomed grips with the gods and galloping consumption; the sounds with which any host of Dylan's was bound to become familiar, sooner rather than later. Perhaps in their way these sounds were comparable with the strange cries of a bird of paradise or the stridulation of certain courting spiders: for they were a fantastically developed evolution of the noises a small boy will make who doesn't want to go to school any more than Dylan wanted to face returning consciousness, inwit, and the day—who wants to impress his solicitous earth-mother, in the hope that his illness will be recognized and he will be sent back to bed and cosseted. So Dylan tried to beg of reality a reprieve from the sun and the consciousness of wasted time.

But there was no reprieve and the groans and the coughing diminished in anguish and volume as he descended to the ground floor and the kitchen. There he found my wife frying New Zealand oyster fritters for his breakfast. He was reassured that he was sufficiently human for someone to feel him worth cooking for, even if or perhaps because it wasn't his wife or mother. Perhaps he wasn't after all such a monster, a spendthrift, lecher, drunkard, brute. He ate the fritters as fast as they came out of the pan, chewed his rinds of bacon and turned up his eyes, lost himself in a fresh role of hungry and grateful guest, an accepted and pardoned reprobate, and as the blood sugar returned to his veins, cheered up and forgot his woes and set out to entertain my wife in return with wit and anecdote.

Eventually my wife and he set off for the Eastgate where at

lunchtime I found them with Louis MacNeice and Bertie Rodgers all in splendid form. It was something of a struggle to persuade Dylan when it was time to leave but we duly got him to the railway station and on to the train to London for his early afternoon broadcast.

Our Saturday morning headquarters by this time had become the back bar of the Lamb and Flag—we left the front bar to C. S. Lewis and to Henry Whitehead and his coterie of mathematicians. Margaret Taylor whom we had lately met at Joyce Cary's and who had discovered our partiality for Dylan used to drop in and keep us informed of his adventures and if Dylan himself were in Oxford he came also. But his preferred pub was the bar of the George, partly because of its comparative proximity to the railway station. He did not live to see its ultimate degraded fate: to be taken over and incorporated into the premises of a bank.

In those days I often used the George restaurant upstairs for business lunches and would usually find Dylan and his wife and friends installed when I went to meet my own guests in the downstairs bar. On one such occasion after he had stayed the night with us I was surprised to observe that he was wearing a shirt I recognized as mine, a blue one. But I was appeased on returning home that evening to find he had left behind a dirty one of much better quality after my wife had surrendered mine. On another day I was for some reason or other wearing a hat, a rather extraordinary blue felt hat I had picked up in Paris and one to which I was deeply attached; perhaps because it was the only hat I had ever found which my wife thought suited me. I left it in the bar while I went upstairs to lunch. When I called back again after lunch I was surprised to see it stowed away in an open bag Dylan had with him for his visit that afternoon to London. I insisted on reclaiming it, rather to his chagrin. He explained that Caitlin thought it suited him and it was the only hat he had. I did not risk asking her if it suited me also but replied that my wife thought it did and it was the only hat I had. I might as well have given in at once. For the next time we met in the George the same thing happened, only this time I didn't notice till he got away. And when I inquired later about the hat's fate, with even some faint hope of getting it back, he explained that he had left it on the rack of his compartment while he went to the restaurant car and in his absence some unscrupulous bastard had swiped it; no doubt someone who didn't have a hat and who thought his wife would think it suited him.

Some time in the spring of 1949 Dylan heard from friends that the Boat House in Laugharne was up for sale. It was in Laugharne that he had first met Caitlin and after they were married they had lived for a while in a place that overlooked the Strand and the Boat House. Dylan was eager to go back to Wales and to this special place in Wales, Caitlin perhaps less so. Margaret Taylor once again showed her generosity and bought the Boat House so that Dylan might be again where he was most at home and able to write his poetry. As he was hoping to make some money out of film scripts the idea was that he should pay rent, an idea which —like money to be earned from writing for films—seems to have come to nothing.

The move to Laugharne was in May and from then on encounters with Dylan became less frequent, since he had fewer occasions to be in Oxford. Now and then he did turn up on one mission or another and we had drinks; once at least, I recall, in the Turf, with Norman Cameron whom I had not previously met and whose poetry we all admired.

One night in late October that year I seemed to have for once a clear evening in front of me and had just settled into my study to write an overdue article on the New Zealand writer Frank Sargeson when the telephone rang. It was Dylan. He was over at the Victoria with Bernard Gutteridge and a young friend of theirs who was known to be rich and had literary leanings. They were on their way to Wales in the friend's car but were running late and so, I suppose to run later, they had stopped in Oxford for a drink. Would I come over?

I abandoned Frank, of course, or rather deferred him, and went across to the local, my wife joining us later. Afterwards we came back home with a bottle of gin. The friend, whom I was meeting for the first time, produced various goodies from the boot of his car, including chicken in aspic and a bottle of champagne. This was not the standard of fare I associated with Dylan: if he ate at all when he was away from home it was usually an indifferently munched sandwich in a pub or a sausage or a piece of bread and cheese.

This time, at any rate, Dylan was prepared to eat and he was in his best form, having drunk but not being drunk. He had been making a selection of poems with a view to reading them on the visit he was to make to America the following year. So his mind was resonant with verse and before long he was standing at the mantelpiece reading his favourites to us. His reading of the Hardy poems stands out best in my memory. Reading Hardy to myself I had always spoken him in my mind's ear in a rather flat, un-inflected way, which I took to be appropriate to his general tone. But in Dylan's reading the grey, somewhat ashen quality I asso-ciated with Hardy vanished, and the poems were breathed on and became fiery coals. One of the poems was 'After a Journey'. It was a favourite of Louis MacNeice's, though Louis used to shake his head over the innocence that allowed Hardy to write the line 'And the unseen waters' ejaculations awe me'. That hurdle gave no difficulty to the exalted vaulting of Dylan's voice. He read on, poem after poem of Hardy's, until at the ending of the final one— alas, I have forgotten which—he burst into tears, too moved to go on.

Next day I find I noted in my diary: 'Dylan is very emotional but like a good Welshman also very suspicious. Thus when he has expressed himself very warmly, in fact exposed himself, he will suddenly react violently towards a self-sneering cynicism. It imparts a curious rhythm to his talk.' This remark was prompted in part by the conversation that followed the reading. It now became clear that Dylan, Bernard, and others were hoping that their rich young friend would finance a new journal, to be called *Circus*, which John Davenport was to edit. The ostensible reason for their descent on me this particular evening was to persuade me to become a contributor but I felt an uneasy suspicion that they were trying to impress the potential angel by their intimacy with a respectable publisher. For the talk seemed to be at one level a rational discussion of publishing possibilities but on another level it had an element of the conspiratorial from which the potential patron, by his youth and simplicity and by the fact that it was his money at stake, was somehow excluded. I felt as if I were being made, however uncomfortably, an accessory to something of which I didn't quite approve. I temporized on the question of contributing a story and my diary notes: 'We shall see. But I felt sorry for ——, a child among veterans of the literary jungle and, it seems, a rich child at that.'

In the end, they all stayed the night. We went to bed late and I was off to the office in the morning as usual before any of the others were up. We were to meet in the Victoria before lunch for a farewell drink. I was there on time and found only Dylan, standing morosely alone at the bar, with a pint of beer before him. 'Little chits of girls,' he was grumbling aloud but apparently to himself. 'Little chits of girls.' 'What's the matter, Dylan?' I asked. 'Little chits of girls,' he said. 'A man spends his whole life and strength and energy trying to write poetry and a little chit of a girl, no more than five years old, comes and does it better with no trouble at all. "I eat the wind", indeed. That's my kind of line, that it might take me a whole day to write.'

From his confused explanation and my wife's questioning of our daughter Delia we were able to reconstruct what had happened. Dylan had got up late, after the others had gone out, and was standing looking glumly out of the window when Delia came in from school. 'Are you the man with the poems in his head?' she had asked. Dylan turned from the window and looked at her with his solemn bulging brown eyes and had admitted that he had poems in his head. 'I have a poem in my head, too,' Delia said. 'You have, have you? And what is it?'

> 'I eat the wind,
> And I drink the rain.'

I got Dylan to the corner table with another pint of bitter, others came in, the story was repeated but this time with chuckling admiration, for Dylan was easily mollified and always generous. And not long afterwards they vanished into Wales. I toyed for a while with the idea of getting Dylan to edit an anthology on the lines of the pieces he had collected for reading but guessed that he would never submit to the drudgery of getting it ready for press. It would be a matter of paying some huge advance and ending up without a manuscript. And, besides, it would not necessarily be a service to Dylan to distract him from his own work into thorny paths of editorship for which he was not temperamentally fitted.

A month or two followed in which all I heard of Dylan was the usual distant rumbling of rumour in the city. Then on 19 December a mutual friend rang: Dylan had been in London the previous week, on one of his excursions from Laugharne. He had lost the only copy of a new poem, notes for it and all, passport and briefcase. He couldn't even remember what pubs he had been in, so there was no hope of tracing what he had lost. He was broke and had no money to buy Christmas presents for his wife and children. Everyone else, including the friend, was broke for the time being. Could I lend the friend £20 to give to Dylan and be paid back after Christmas? I was hard up myself in those days and £20 was a lot of money to me. But I agreed to raise it and hand it over in the Lamb and Flag the following Saturday. It could then be got to Dylan in time for Christmas.

I duly handed over the cheque that Saturday and then became immersed in my own Christmas arrangements. My wife had gone off the preceding month on a visit to New Zealand. A Danish friend of ours, Elizabeth, and her daughter, were staying with us, and Elizabeth and I were determined to make the Christmas almost as good for the children as if my wife were not away.

Where Dylan and his family in fact spent Christmas I don't now remember, I think with the Davenports in London. But three days after Christmas they appeared in the Victoria. Would I put them up for a day or two? I consulted Elizabeth and she readily agreed. The day or two stretched out into a week. Caitlin and Dylan seemed very happy to be together—they had left the children with friends or relations. After they went to bed the first night, about midnight and much earlier than usual, Dylan came down again to ask if I had any spare jerseys. He and Caitlin didn't wear pyjamas, it seemed, but liked to wear jerseys. I dug out some old rugger jerseys, a light blue one I had used in the days when I played for Otago University and a Balliol one in red and white horizontal stripes. They wore these every night for the rest of their stay, Caitlin the blue and Dylan the striped, and Elizabeth used to be amused and touched when she brought them breakfast in the attic to see them both sitting up in the double bed in their jerseys, as hungry as little boys.

I enjoyed their stay though towards the end my diary begins its characteristic grumbles. 'Dylan is as good company as ever and I got to like his wife. But neither of them are very good guests since they carry with them a cloud of uncertainty about times of coming and going, eating, etc., and the presence of someone to talk to is a considerable temptation to me to stay up late and drink too much. Also they are often attended by vitality-parasites and that is tiresome.'

We spent most evenings after supper in the Victoria. It was the time of the Korean War and Dylan was somewhat obsessed with this, as indeed were most of us then. It upset him as much as did the Rosenberg case later, when I can remember him declaiming with genuine anguish and compassion about the iniquity of capital punishment, no matter what the crime.

These evenings in the pub usually got difficult towards the end. As it was my local I was in some sense master of ceremonies. My own friends could on the whole be relied on for tact and a quick intuition of social situations. The same was not always true of Dylan's friends—the sort of people, too many of them, who are able to take but not to give, and who end by draining.

Caitlin, I guess, was in any case dreading the time, not far away now, of Dylan's departure for America, and felt in her bones that no good would come of it. She tended, when in the pub, to become distant, remote, hostile even. An uneasiness would spread out from her and it was difficult to know which of us was provoking it. We would try to keep some sort of conversation going and Elizabeth the Dane was very good. Herself a painter, she had an instinctive sympathy for the suppressed artist in Caitlin and liked her as a woman—liked her better, I think, than she liked Dylan, which was not what usually happened.

Dylan, nervously aware of the tension, no doubt much more aware of its reasons, would show this only by putting on his very best pub form. The others were happy enough to be totally under the spell. But Caitlin, after all, had heard all the stories, even in a way those that Dylan was that moment for the first time improvising. It was no doubt this very display of the verbal bower-bird that had first attracted her to him. But now the courtship was as much for others as for her, and for others whom she somewhat unfairly but naturally enough despised. So Caitlin, at the end of the table nearest the door usually and furthest away from Dylan, emanated a formidable discontent, unhappiness even.

You could feel her first trying to abstract herself completely, be somewhere else in her mind. Or she would watch me and the others with cold dislike whenever she thought we were not aware of it: I could feel an intense, baleful beam of hostility directed against myself. In her eyes I was a bourgeois, one of those who whatever happened kept himself safe against the worst guilt and remorse, against being moneyless and homeless, a dependent on others; and yet one of those who tried to have it both ways by letting Dylan be their proxy at the sharp extremes of experience, by listening to him and encouraging him to drink too much, make himself a motley to the view, spend on us the strength and energy he should have reserved for himself, his poetry, and her.

There was too much truth in this for my comfort and I was a silent assistant prosecutor in her silent accusations. It seemed to me that the enormous development in Dylan's poetry since his marriage owed almost everything to her and his life with her. She was entitled to be a strict and jealous guardian. Yet in the end everyone, man or woman, must be his own guardian. If he were not here, with us, he would be in another pub, with other people, less vigilant on his behalf than I was. For he needed this escape sometimes from his devouring poetic self into an easier social life. Our endorsements of his self-confidence might seem to Caitlin cheap, and too easily won, but none the less they were what he from time to time needed. And if it was his weaker self that needed them, that self was still part of the whole self that went to make the poet. No one but Dylan himself was entitled to adjudicate between the claims, and if he judged wrongly it must still be his judgement.

Still, by the same reasoning, I was myself responsible for what I did and could not escape qualms lest my rationalizing be wrong and there were not some other course which I might adopt. Meanwhile, too, I was accountable in Caitlin's eyes on another charge: for I like so many others had now become a host and so, owing to Dylan's improvidence, she was obliged to me also for food and shelter when she wanted to be obliged to no one.

Her real attention, however, was for Dylan. It was not that she was enjoying his talk. The better he talked the more one felt she hated it and, for the time being, him, as only a woman can hate the man she loves. He ought to be more proud, as she was proud, and not debase himself by relishing so much the rapt attention of a crowd of people who were good for nothing but the inflation of his vanity, exploiting his vanity to make him dissipate his strength in amusing them, when it was she who would have to console next morning his groans over the expanse of spirit in a waste of shame.

She may have felt, too, an element of the creative artist's jealousy. For she was not only a beautiful woman, very much a woman, she was a frustrated dancer as well. Dancing was her art, even though life with Dylan, love for him and sacrifice to him, had thwarted her as a dancer. If he had not been here in this pub, if we were different people, she might have been able to dance, herself the centre of herself and of people's attention. Or if they had been alone together, and she felt like it, she could have danced for him.

I may have been wrong in so reading her feelings, for I could not be sure of reading rightly the feelings of women I knew far better than I ever knew Caitlin, but my apprehensions used to mount as the evening wore on. For I sensed in her one of those socially fearless people who will ruthlessly do whatever they have a mind to, however unconventional or embarrassing for others. I did not fear Caitlin particularly but I did fear scenes, and do. And I knew that if it crossed her mind to do so she was capable of doing or saying something appalling. To that extent I was certainly a bourgeois. So I would watch her warily and this I am sure she sensed but for some reason or other she never exploited my social cowardice and the feared explosion never took place.

At the end of their stay they went back to London and John Davenport who was writing to me about a short story I sent for *Circus*—it proved too long and was eventually published in *Arena*, while *Circus* itself folded after three or four issues—reported they were staying with him and sent their love. Shortly afterwards Dylan set off for America.

I am not sure whether it was before or after this first visit to America that he was interviewed by the BBC for a possible regular job as replacement for Louis MacNeice in the Features Department, Louis having gone off to represent the British Council in Athens. The night before the interview he turned up at the flat of a friend of mine looking for a bed. She put him up and the next morning had the problem of making him look presentable. She decided that his shirt was dirty enough to disqualify him. She tried turning it inside out in the hope that the collar reversed would pass as clean. But Dylan had managed to get it dirty on that side too. There wasn't time or money to buy another—shirts were always a problem for so vagrant a poet—so she decided he would have to wear a cravat instead and gave him the pick of hers. With that radar sense of quality that governed his taste in poetry and other people's clothes, he chose her own favourite scarf. Whether because the BBC did not share their taste or because they knew Dylan would never succeed at even pretending to be a bureaucrat, he did not get the job. Nor did she ever see her scarf again.

I saw Dylan a little in the pubs after his return from the United States that May, and heard more. His friends were deeply concerned both for him and Caitlin because of a serious love affair in which he had become involved while in New York. But I could not believe that his relationship with Caitlin, however deeply troubled, could be seriously in danger. Whatever his faults he did not seem to me to be a man who could throw overboard something that was so profound, and I knew he was deeply attached to his children.

In the spring of 1952 I was myself in New York on business. Late one night I came away with two friends, an Englishman and an American, from a party in Greenwich Village. The Englishman suggested we call at the White Horse Tavern, reputed to resemble an English pub. We were sitting at a table in a corner and drinking a very un-English English-type pint, when there was a sudden irruption of newcomers: a few girls, George Reavey, Ruthven Todd, and, in the rear, Dylan himself. We joined forces for a while and the illusion of being back in the Soho of years before was almost complete. But that was the talk of Dylan, master of illusion, rather than the physical ambience.

He was busy that summer, back from America, writing the Prologue to his *Collected Poems*. When this was finished he took it to London to show Louis MacNeice, one of the few whose judgement he valued, Vernon Watkins being another. They spent an evening together and Louis first read Dylan a poem of his. Dylan had only one shocked comment. 'Louis, you've used the word "pub" in a poem!' For Dylan, when he was writing high poetry, always wrote in his Sunday-best language, as if he were a priest celebrating a High Mass of literature.

Then Louis listened while Dylan read the Prologue. At the end Louis admired it but Dylan was not satisfied. 'But what did you think of the rhyme scheme? Did you like it?' 'Was it a rhymed poem?' Louis asked. And once again Dylan was shocked. If Louis's fine and discerning ear failed to register the rhyme scheme, whose could?

So exacting was Dylan in matters of his craft. Yet most of us would not notice the rhyme scheme, even reading the poem with the eye, without the help which Dylan gave his publisher when he sent in the MS. and which he also found it tactfully expedient to give in a letter to Vernon Watkins. For the poem was divided into two long parts, each of fifty-one lines. And the first part rhymes forwards, the second part backwards, until they meet in the middle where the last rhyme of the first part rhymes with the first line of the second. One gets the impression from the self-disparaging tone of his explanations that he was proud of his virtuosity but puzzled to know why it had chosen this particular

occasion and mode to display itself. I believe that it was his dae-
mon, his genius, that had taken over and compelled him to a
dazzling feat somehow most fitting for his last considerable poem,
one that is a fitting epilogue, though technically a prologue, to
all the others he saw fit to select for survival, and a poem that
gives the lie to the legend of his failing powers.

I saw him from time to time in London in that and the following year, 1953. It was in this last of his years, I think, that I saw
him for the last time. He was staying the night with us in Oxford.
After we came back from the Victoria, he stood once more by
the mantelpiece, but this time to talk and not to recite Hardy. He
was in a somewhat sombre mood and, looking down to where I
sat secure in my ambience and my armchair, he was pitying himself
because he would never reach the age of forty. I refused to sym-
pathize and proved to his incredulity, almost to the point of
huffiness, that I was his elder by a year. I had every intention,
come hell or high water, of becoming forty by 1 September, and
saw no reason why he should not follow me in that almost autonomic achievement in October 1954. The child in him was miffed
at my having the better of him in age but I hesitate now to say
that it was the child in him that was so profoundly and tragically
convinced that he would die before he was forty.

Why he was so convinced I do not know. Certainly death was
an obsession with him always, and the frailness, the insecurity, of
life. He was given to telling stories of how his lungs had haemor-
rhaged, delighting in his descriptions of the flooding blood and
the horror and sympathy they evoked. He would often croak
sepulchrally about his doomed, cirrhotic liver and his fits of
vomiting, his frequent anorexia, made it all credible. Yet, when
the tragic eyes were lifted from one and the actor's voice no
longer bemused, I rather assumed that these were exaggerations,
attempts by one of the Dylans one had come to know, to translate
the guilt and remorse of hangovers into genuine physical maladies
for which he could legitimately entreat solicitude. As a small child,
one gathered, he had been 'delicate' and had spent a lot of time ill
in bed, and one suspected his mother had welcomed these oppor-
tunities to envelop and cherish him, to spoil him.

Since he was small and competitive this would have produced a double reaction: on the one hand, whenever his fecklessness and recklessness had got him into some hopeless mess, he would try to retreat into the childhood refuge of ill health and accept cosseting from whoever was ready to give it. On the other hand, it looks as if he attempted to compensate for this pattern of early weakness by trying to outdo the other boys, and later other men, in the extravagance of the demands he made upon himself and his physique. He was determined to be one of the boys, to excel as a young dog, to smoke and drink and shock more than any of the other young dogs.

To behave in this way, however, for someone like Dylan, is to repress but not to suppress a disapproving sensibility, an imagination which discerns how others, the victims of inconsiderateness, must feel. So the sensibility and imagination reinforce the conscience, already hypertrophied by a puritan upbringing. When the outer aggression slackens, from exhaustion or boredom, such a conscience grabs the chance to remind its owner that he is making himself a physiological calamity and a moral scarecrow, the text for a hell-fire sermon. So—like Samuel Bennet (an echo of Sam Beckett?) in *Adventures in the Skin Trade* who weeps even as he savagely destroys his family's most cherished penates— Dylan was able at once to behave outrageously and shudder with remorse and a sense of the nemesis to follow. And that exquisite thrill in the end became an addiction. Impending doom became necessary to the pleasure of the moment and communicated itself inevitably through his poetry. So that he saw his poems as 'statements on the way to a grave', felt himself forever toiling 'towards the ambush of his wounds', and was never long unaware of 'the voyage towards ruin I must run'.

In adult life the drive towards the extreme, for he could do nothing by quarters and never drank a half, meant that when he was not at home writing poetry, one and the most intense pole of his being, he was in the pubs among the hard men. And hard men they were, iron men as long as they lasted: people like Roy Campbell, John Davenport, Louis MacNeice, Bertie Rodgers, Julian Maclaren-Ross, to name only those whose iron is now rusting in the grave.

No one has better brought out what Dylan himself had to give than Louis MacNeice in *Autumn Sequel*: not so much the quality of iron man but the contribution of life and enjoyment that entered with him into a bar and welled as it seemed inexhaustibly from his exuberant and witty and humorous imagination:

> The bars are open and a bright light glares
>
> On brass and glass and bottle, the world is wet,
> Gwilym has come to town, it is time to take
> Our kindness, blindness, double. Yet. And yet?
>
> This is the first of September; let us unmake
> The dreary dog days and baptize the Fall,
> The winds that exhilarate, the gold that drops in the lake.
>
> Gwilym begins: with the first pint a tall
> Story froths over, demons from the hills
> Concacchinate in the toilet, a silver ball
>
> Jumps up and down in his beer till laughter spills
> Us out to another bar followed by frogs
> And auks and porpentines and armadills.
>
> For Gwilym is a poet; analogues
> And double meanings crawl behind his ears
> And his brown eyes were scooped out of the bogs,
>
> A jester and a bard. Archaic fears
> Dog him with handcuffs but this rogue's too quick,
> They grab and he turns a cartwheel and disappears.

But this desire to please, and this power of pleasing, this happiness Dylan found in the release of the saloon bar and alcohol and in the company of other writers and men who could appreciate his marvellous social powers, these were the cause of many of his difficulties. Hence came the tendency to put off, to defer for the sake of present pleasure, and Dylan's kind of vitality lives so richly in the present that tomorrow exists not for what has to be done but only as a sinister shadow which will, when it comes, enforce contemplation of time now being wasted and is therefore to be dreaded and deferred. 'Procrastination is an element in which I live.' As if he were a frozen salamander, delighting in an icy fire of stillness. So came about the failures to do things that would have satisfied conscience and creditors, would have earned money and spared him those desperate self-abasements of the borrower who knows he won't repay and knows his friends know. And sometimes also the reaction against those friends, friends who lent him money, lent him company and ears, but stole his time and his peace of mind, the reaction we glimpse in 'To Others Than You':

> . . . though I loved them for their faults
> As much as for their good,
> My friends were enemies on stilts
> With their heads in a cunning cloud.

Both as a poet and as a man Dylan needed an intense life, a life of drama, and he could not get it entirely from within himself; for, however egoist, he was no solipsist but affectionate, gregarious. People and alcohol, people and improvidence, will always provide drama, as will obligations readily accepted and recklessly ignored. Thus his marriage was begun as an idyll of babes in the wood but he would not always recognize that the idyll must change when the babes had babies and the child must become father to the father. But some part of him must have found that in the drama he needed the guilt was an essential part of the plot, in a sense as much craved for as the drama proper. For his own awfulness, his own most desperate derelictions, were a theme to which the preacher in him rose with more passion, more *hwyll*, than any sins of others. They challenged him to some of his best letters in which he writes with an almost lyric passion of abasement and remorse, helped perhaps by the sense that in wrongdoing, too, sins of omission and commission, he excelled all his friends and by the fact that whatever he felt at a given moment, he thought he felt for ever; so that his private times of hell had the additional dimension of eternity.

Alcohol had other attractions, especially for a lyric poet who must always fear that his gift, like a woman's beauty, will not survive its menopause. It can provide osmoses between fact and fantasy, unusual sequences, bizarre disjunctions and leaps of association. For a poet like Dylan, whose dialectic depended on a constant counterpoint and suspension of the antithetical, these are important and desirable, tipping reality to an unusual angle. A poem by Dylan is an equilibrium of tensions, composed like the atom as a self-contained totality, a highly organized system of opposites in balance to one another, of negatives and positives, so compressed that we can feel the force latent in them and the slightest disturbance or dislocation of the parts, in sound or sense, will cause the whole to fly apart, to fragment like a hand-grenade unpinned. The poetry at its most successful controlled and got its strength from the reconciliation of its contained contradictions.

And so at its best moments, and they were many, did the life. And it is useless to lament that it contained so much unnecessary waste and suffering. For that kind of life, waste and suffering were necessary for that kind of man and that kind of poetry. To ask otherwise would be 'another kettle of wishes', to ask that instead of 'poems in praise of God's world by a man who doesn't believe in God' another man should have given us other poems lacking that basic contradiction from which the true passion and greatness of Dylan's best poetry comes. We cannot have genuine projections of glory and despair without extremity in the life that they reflect, consume, and distil. To see this, one need only consider what it must have been like to spend many days on the writing of a single line of a poem and what sort of man it was who had the compulsion to do this, a man with 'an instinctive delight in the muddled world', and an overwhelming drive to make of the muddle in all its sinful variation a world that was fixed and perfect and forever.

From that unbearable solitude of creation, it is not surprising that when the making fit was over he descended upon the town in much the same way as the bushwhackers of my childhood after twelve months' desperately hard work in the back of beyond came down into the city and consumed their money and their strength in a wild fling before returning to the wilderness.

One question still teases: Dylan's poems, so difficult to the understanding of the eye, and yet so apparently a cerebration as well as a celebration of life, became far more easily intelligible when read aloud by Dylan himself. How far do poems, composed with the aid of the voice and such a voice as his, the ear at times the final test before the copingstone of a word was finally lowered into place, how far do such poems need the human voice which was so vital to their composition if they are to be properly felt and comprehended?

Perhaps the answer may be that Dylan was himself an anachronism, a throwback to the medieval religious past, a bard born out of his time. Had he been a court poet in medieval Wales all would have been right for him. He would have been entitled, in full bardic panoply, to sing in the royal hall his songs in praise of God and the king. He would have been able to eulogize and satirize, to declaim to an assembled audience which recognized and savoured his intricate rhymes, his opulent diction, the wealth of allusion, and the comparatively simple themes. He would have been a Lord of the Word in a world where words were still admitted to be magical and where his own superb voice, the internal harmony of the poems, would have been recognized for what they were, in the seamless culture of a place and time where the first appeal was to the ear and it was accepted that poetry should call on the shared consciousness of a jealously preserved, timeless, and sanctified past.

But Dylan lived in a time when there were no royal patrons, no accepted and traditional place for the poet. The past of the nation was no longer accessible and to revert to a golden age the poet could go back no further than his childhood. The gods and the kings were dead, and had left to his generation only a racking conscience, guilt, and an affluent society where the poet was poor, a democracy of talent where talent did not mean a poet was to be in a place of honour. And the oral had lost its power to bewitch and bemuse except on the juggling tongues of politicians and people did not think when they listened but only when they puzzled in solitude over the written or printed page. A time when the celebrant of life could only be a courtier of death.

Dylan, foreboding like King Arthur his coming death, left us the day after his visit in 1953, taking with him another of my shirts, this time unreplaced, but leaving behind him a leather belt by which my wife still sometimes with a grieving smile measures the girth of that beer-fed and unreturning belly which so often shook with the laughter Dylan evoked in others. We were never to see him again and we were not to know till Louis told us long afterwards how Dylan had blacked out in a bar when they were drinking together that there was a real basis for his dismal apprehensions. Yet he was led on by America, like some tragic hero in a saga who must follow his destiny to his doom, and he was never to see his fortieth year to heaven.

So Caitlin lost her Dylan, and we his friends lost him, and poetry lost one of the great makers. Yet the ball he threw while playing in the park has not yet touched the ground and his poetry will be with us for as long as forever is, until we too have advanced as far as we can go 'in the direction of the elementary town'.

> And did we once see Gwilym plain? We did.
>
> And heard him even plainer. A whole masque
> Of tones and cadences—the organ boom,
> The mimicry, then the chuckles; we could bask
>
> As though in a lush meadow in any room
> Where that voice started, trellising the air
> With honeysuckle or dogrose, bloom on bloom,
>
> And loosing bees between them and a bear
> To grumble after the bees. Such rooms are still
> Open to us but now are merely spare
>
> Rooms and in several senses: damp and chill
> With dust-sheets over the furniture and the voice
> Silent, the meadow vanished, the magic nil.

A Dream Takes Wing

Warsaw, 1938

Brooklyn, 1964

Itzik Manger

7

A Dream Takes Wing

ITZIK MANGER
(1901-1969)

SOME six months after the International P.E.N. Club conference of August 1950 where we first met, Itzik Manger
wrote to me: 'I am still thinking about the peculiar circumstances
of our meeting in Edinburgh, how you came up the first time to
me, from among the busybodies there, telling me that you are
representing New Zealand, and asking me whom I represent and
I told you "Yiddish".

'And so started a friendship with you and other Irish and Scottish writers, an impression I took away with me and I keep it.
You told me that it is the first time you have been present at such
a meeting, and you do not want any more! I, too, was for the
first time at such a congress and I hope it is the last time.'

After so long I now find it difficult to remember why I did
attend the conference. Perhaps I thought I might meet someone
interesting and new—improbable as I was then getting on for forty
and not by temperament sanguine. Most likely, the invitation had
reached me far enough in advance for me to think that I ought to
go, if only to save New Zealand from sending someone especially
all that long distance or from not being represented at all; for
most New Zealand writers now lived at home and I was among
the last of the expatriates. Anyway I had accepted and was captive
to the obligation.

I am glad now, because it was the occasion of my coming to know Itzik. We were billeted, I seem to remember, in some hostel quite a long way from the centre of Edinburgh, in a suburb. I was sitting by myself that first Friday evening, though not exactly alone, in the small reception lobby, cursing myself for having come, wondering where I could get a drink in a real bar, watching late arrivals collect their papers at the conference office and self-important people trying to establish their identity in the usual ways—asking for better rooms, inquiring in voices meant to carry if there were any messages for them from Sir Compton Mackenzie, Eric Linklater, Lord Crawford, or the like. It was soon enough after the war for me to be reminded of first nights in new barracks, a new Orderly Room, a new Officers' Mess; and, still further back, of being a new boy at school, a first-year student in Otago University, a first-year undergraduate in Balliol. Perhaps change of environment, a sudden shake of the kaleidoscope, was the only experience of newness now possible, since there was little hope of change in oneself, except for the worse: any improvement of behaviour could now come only from loss of appetite, the onset of infirmities, debility of the demon moribund.

A refugee from these dismal thoughts, I opened my own folder of papers listlessly and looked at the list of people attending. There were many literary names familiar to me, few people whom I would have recognized by sight, two or three whom I knew and liked but not sharing this particular billet. I guessed that they, and the great men one might have liked to look upon, would have cried off at the last moment, as is the way of things. I tried to persuade myself to fix the conference button to my lapel but could not harden myself against a schoolboy shame of wearing a badge of identity, even though admitting it would have been sensible; an inhibition I had retained from New Zealand, like being unable to carry an umbrella.

I became aware of a small, slightly built, and very 'Jewish-looking' man in a shabby dark suit, a man thin to the point of being cadaverous. He was stalking to and fro across the lobby, muttering occasionally to himself, and he seemed to radiate an

extraordinary combination of energy and anguish. He was arrest-
ing, I could not see quite why. Perhaps because of this sombre
and almost feverish radiation, perhaps because of his very large
and burning dark eyes. Yet I had seen plenty of dark-eyed Jews
since coming to Europe fifteen years before, many of them un-
happy, agitated, tragic often, though usually because of the things
that had happened to them, been done to them, rather than
because of something in themselves.

I was of an age when one is already wary of other people's
drama and frugal of the exactions it makes on one's energy, the
demand for sympathy which will almost certainly follow intervention. The grinding blackmail of self-pity, a haemophilia of
selfishness which I had by now come to recognize would always
be draining me, made me feel that my resources of energy must
be jealously husbanded, and not lightly diverted to others. This
was not always easy, since I had been unable to kill a stubborn
curiosity about my fellow creatures and still found myself, taken
off guard, actually feeling sympathy for them. Deserving cases
were the most dangerous. On the whole, however, the Levite in
me was learning to get the better of the Samaritan.

Yet this man was compelling. He looked lonely and that was
something I could identify with. But the lonely fear the lonely,
lest their united condition become a compound deterrent to
would-be rescuers. I was drawn now more by that something in
his presence which suggested a power, a force, not a power of the
world but a power within the self. He was the first such man I had
seen for a long time. I decided to overcome my own shyness and
speak to him. After all, he was obviously a lonely and distraught
Jew and most of us felt in some way guilty towards Jews, even
those of us who had shed Nazi blood in their cause, even a simple
New Zealander who had never heard of anti-Semitism till Hitler,
never seen it until in the Mosley riots I watched a mounted
police sergeant lead his patrol through an East End street, holding
his nostrils closed with the thumb and forefinger of his left hand
to show what he thought of those stinking Yids.

I got up and shortened my step to keep pace alongside the
stranger. He presumably knew no English, so I identified myself

in clumsy French. He stopped and turned to inspect me, his eyes dark and large with what seemed to be amazement at being addressed by someone he did not know. But he replied in English which at least was better than my French, gave a name I had difficulty in catching, and explained courteously enough, and with a certain pride, that he was a delegate for Yiddish literature, in particular Yiddish drama.

There was a pause then while I hesitated for something to say. My knowledge of Yiddish was a mere rag of remembered philology and I knew nothing of its literature except that there had been a Yiddish theatre in Russia and my Jewish Communist friends used to point to it as evidence of how there was no anti-Semitism in the Socialist Sixth of the World. Presumably this stranger's knowledge of New Zealand literature was at least as exiguous, with more excuse.

'Will there be whisky at this reception we are going to?' the stranger asked in a voice of passionate anxiety and with so thick an accent that for a moment I thought he meant he would not go if there was. But then I saw I was wrong. Such anxiety could never be felt from religious conviction but only by a man who needed whisky and needed it soon. My heart went out to him in double sympathy, for I too would have been glad of a glass and I knew enough to know that at the kind of reception we were going to, as guests of the Scottish P.E.N., there would be no whisky.

'No,' I explained, drawing on a grim experience of receptions that went back as far as Dunedin twenty years before. 'There will be claret cup and there will be orange juice.'

'What is claret cup?'

'It is a drink made with a very little claret and a great deal of fruit juice. It is always made by the women, a bad mistake. And the older the women, the more fruit juice and the less claret. Especially if they are older Edinburgh ladies. These ones will be.'

He looked like a man sentenced to death. Foreigner he might be, but he fully understood the gravity of what I had said, and he had not been misled by my off-hand tone. We understood each other.

He said nothing but continued to look into my eyes with anguish and despair.

'Come with me,' I said. 'I will find a place where there is whisky.'

'But we all have to go in a bus. I have a friend who is looking after me and he doesn't like whisky.'

'Too bad about him. Wait a minute and I'll get a taxi.'

In practical matters he was obviously used to being led. Such people may be expected to revolt from time to time but for the moment he was prepared to surrender independence. He followed me to the telephone, like a child following his father to a promise, or a promised land.

I asked the taxi driver to take us to George Heriot's School where the reception was to be held, on the soldierly principle of first reconnoitring one's assigned objective. There was still half an hour or so in hand before the affair was due to begin. When I had paid off the taxi, I put another principle into action: in strange territory always go over the ground on foot. You then remember the way back. So we cast up and down a few side streets until we came upon what seemed like a promising pub.

It was called the Bell Inn, a name of favourable auspice since it recalled a reliable brand of Scotch. Inside, it was beautifully kept in the way pubs used to be kept before there were brewers' mergers, brewers' interior decorators, plastic seats and plastic sandwiches, chemical beer forced out of bogus kegs, managers instead of publicans, and all the other abominations. I ordered a large Bell's for my friend and a pint of 'heavy' for myself, being aware of the Scottish idiosyncrasy by which light beer is 'heavy' and dark beer 'light'.

After that first drink we moved to first names. His was Itzik, and I was now able to establish unobtrusively the surname that I had heard uncertainly when met. So, Itzik Manger. He was insatiably curious about everything round him, why this was called that, what sort of people the other drinkers in the bar might be, details of drinking protocol. I enlightened him as best I could and gently moved to questions about himself. I wanted some sort of evidence, I suppose, to confirm a strong intuition that I had come across a genius. He told me, simply enough and with the same innocent and candid pride I had noticed earlier, that he wrote poems and short stories in Yiddish, and plays, and that until the Germans had exterminated the Jewish peoples of eastern Europe he had been well known from Romania right across to Poland.

Reserving these matters for some more favourable time, we then began to talk of writing in general and soon I recognized that he was a natural lord of language, even in the rather odd English he had picked up during the ten years he had spent in this country. We passed quickly to anecdotes and stories and I was delighted to find that he was a first-rate raconteur who was able to act out his stories with gesture and mimicry. And the stories themselves were always told from a very special angle—a strange innocence of vision, childlike almost, even when the facts related could never have come within the experience of a child. And although his language was always fundamentally simple the metaphors and figures with which he abounded were strange, simultaneously evoking the Bible, the farmyards of my childhood, and the idiom of surrealism so remote from either of these.

Time passed even more rapidly than time usually passes in pubs. Itzik was enjoying himself and so was I. But I am conditioned to regard enjoyment warily as soon as I become conscious of it: its abolition of the future tense is apt to bring unpleasant consequences. I remembered the reception. For all I knew, Itzik's presence might be vital for the future of Yiddish literature, for his own future, whereas my presence or absence was of no importance for my future, much less the future of New Zealand writing. Not trusting pub clocks, even Scottish ones, I checked with my watch and the pub clock said 'I told you so'. The reception must have been going for a good half-hour at least. It was time for us to be off.

Itzik dissented. We were happy here. We might not be happy elsewhere. It was most improbable that we would be happy at the reception. But his friends, his fellow delegates, might be looking for him? He did not care. They were all busybodies, bureaucrats, functionaries, middlemen, apparatchiks, they weren't real writers. It was better here. I changed my tack. It would be impolite to our

Scottish hosts. And they would think the delegate for Yiddish drama had been discourteous. That did it.

We went back by the route I had reconnoitred. The hall was crowded but the ladies of the committee were zealous, ubiquitous. They carried trays on which there was a choice of claret cup or orange juice. Itzik looked at me and we each took a glass of claret cup. I sipped mine with neither surprise nor pleasure. Itzik's mouth puckered and he seemed to have difficulty in not spitting.

> 'Scale of dragon, tooth of wolf,
> Witches' mummy, maw and gulf
> Of the ravin'd salt-sea shark—'

This was a comment on the beverage which I didn't expect him to understand and I paused belatedly when I realized where the quotation was leading. But I underrated my man. He carried the verse on:

> 'Root of hemlock digg'd i' the dark,
> Liver of blaspheming Jew.'

He began to talk about Shakespeare, Shylock, Marlowe and *The Jew of Malta* with the detachment and discrimination of a poet and I admired him more than ever. But at this point the fellow delegate who had been looking for him came up. Not wishing to be present at possible recriminations I drifted off, peering at the labels on people's lapels, circumambulating knotty conversationalists, picking off the occasional bit of smoked salmon and brown bread, trying to postpone the unpleasant need for another dose of claret cup. The noise was deafening.

I met a friend, a Catholic journalist, a convert. He was fond of inside jokes and it was only a few days since the Feast of the Assumption. 'Why is the Pope the greatest of logicians?' I did my best: 'Because he vindicates the ways of God to man?' 'No, you fool, the Supreme Pontiff, not Alexander.' 'Well, then?' 'Because he can make a dogma out of an assumption.' I looked around for Itzik.

He was standing beside me, not carrying a glass. 'What do they mean, talking about export royalty? Is it a plot against the royal family?' He hardly listened to my explanation, even if he could have heard it. That tragic look was back in his eyes.

'Why are we not going back to the Bell Inn?' he asked when I paused. 'There is whisky. I don't like claret cup. It is too much noise here.'

I persuaded him to eat something from one of the trays and then we slipped quietly away. Within a few minutes we were back in a more genuine ambience, a more ancient tradition, of civil Scots drinking decent civil whisky. So must Robert Burns have slipped away many a time from genteel Edinburgh drawing-rooms.

'I thought it was the goy who was supposed to be the shicker,' I said. 'Isn't that your proverb?'

'Where did you learn it?'

I told him. A 'shicker' was a drunk in the New Zealand slang of my boyhood and American Jewish friends in Balliol before the war had told me the saying. He was delighted that I knew at least two words of Yiddish. But it was not his favourite truism.

Soon I realized that he had another gift: he could make friends. It was part of some fearlessness in him, an openness to others, a confidence that disarmed. By the time closing time was called, every regular in that bar—and regulars are normally suspicious of strangers—knew him and had exchanged drinks with him. They made him an honorary Scot and christened him MacManger. Songs had been sung and I was no less surprised than the rest to find that Itzik could quote Burns.

In the following days the Bell Inn became our headquarters and our refuge. A few friends had by now turned up who shared our inability to tolerate more than a little of the interminably fluent rhetoric of Indians and Latins on the principles of the arts, illustrated by copious quotations from national literary heroes in execrable translation or unintelligible origina' When we had had enough it was to the Bell Inn we fled, to drink quietly and discourse on lesser themes.

I began to piece together something of Itzik's history. He was born in 1901 at Czernowitz. His father was a tailor and, according to Itzik, a humorist, an artist, a master of rhyme. Itzik's mother, the daughter of a mattress maker, had a vast repertory of Yiddish folk-songs and folk-tales. Perhaps because his father was better at making funny speeches and writing funny sketches than making money, it was a house of poverty. It was also a house of poetry and piety. At times they were so poor they all, a family of five, had to live in one room or even a cellar and there was always trouble about the rent. But his father made jokes and his mother sang and they all prayed.

At first, as a small boy, Itzik went to a humble little Yiddish school, then to a state primary school. He was intelligent and so was sent on to the Imperial Gymnasium—this was still the Austrian Empire. But piety towards God and reverence to German-speaking teachers were two different things and he was expelled for mocking his superiors.

In any case another world was tugging at him. As a child he had been allowed to help place the benches in the local Yiddish theatre, to hang around the actors and make himself at home behind the scenes. He became a connoisseur of acting and followed the plays against the text as they were performed, rapt in the world that art revealed to him, the truer than life and often larger. And he was more and more saturated in the Bible and Yiddish folk-lore, the two dominants of the culture he grew up in. During his time at the Austrian school he had become devoted to Goethe and Schiller and Heine and these still gave him a wider perspective, even after he turned more and more back to the lore and language of his origins.

To earn his living he became a journeyman tailor and when the Russians reached Czernowitz not long after the Great War began he moved off to Jassy where he had various jobs and made friends among socialists. By 1918 he was writing in Yiddish and knew that was the tongue of his genius. Ten years or so later his verse had been published in various journals and he went to Warsaw where he quickly became well known. Between then and the beginning of the new war he wandered through Poland and the Baltic countries and Romania, every region of eastern Europe where there were peoples who spoke Yiddish, the culture which nourished his imagination and which he in his turn enriched. He would go from town to town, village to village, reciting traditional stories and poems, and stories and poems of his own, to thousands at fairs and markets, in taverns and in open places, wherever life or business brought people together. It had been a marvellous life, immediate contact with his audience, the sort of instant and mutual reaction known in the west only to the great politicians of the nineteenth century, to a Gladstone or a Daniel O'Connell and perhaps, among writers, to no one but Dickens. For Itzik the people on whose gratitude and hospitality he depended were a reservoir of poetry and tragedy and homely wisdom. Their lives were drama and their language was poetry as language has not been in Europe, except for the Celtic fringe, since the days of Chaucer or of Villon. For in the west all was changed by Caxton and by Luther.

And in the east all was changed, but this time destroyed utterly, by Hitler. Somehow or other Itzik, so little qualified by force or cunning or foresight to escape, survived to become the mourner and memorial of his people. At the time of the invasion of Poland he managed to make his way to Paris. When France was overwhelmed and the Nazis arrived in Paris he got away to Marseilles. He wanted to get to Palestine but had no papers. In despair of finding a passage he was sitting in a waterfront café with some confused notion of getting a job on a ship as a deck hand when a stranger accosted him. 'Why are you looking so bewildered?' The stranger turned out to be a sea captain who was about to run a cargo of ammunition to Oran and was also supplying the British with information about shipping. He took on Itzik as a member of his crew and got him to Gibraltar.

Here Itzik managed to get aboard an English ship, loaded to the scuppers with refugees. He was weak with hunger and ill besides, his strength being that of the spirit rather than the bodily frame. There had been great seas, a confusion of lost people speaking strange tongues. Itzik himself spoke no English, had no possessions, did not know where he was going. But the Scottish captain had somehow found him out from the rest, sensed his quality, and given him a drink out of his own precious bottle of whisky. Water of life it had been to him, Itzik said, and was confirmed in this when I explained to him that from the original Gaelic this was an exact translation.

They had docked in Liverpool. Itzik was very ill and was taken to hospital. Christmas came. He woke on Christmas morning to find his bed full of Christmas presents. Where had they come from? A rabbi had sent them, nurses said. What sort of rabbi could this be, who would bring a poor sick Jew, who knew no one, presents on Christmas Day, of all days? And he realized that the nurses had been sorry for him, alone without family or friends, when everyone else in the ward had presents. So they had bought the presents themselves and invented the story about the rabbi to cheer him up, not guessing how improbable it was. Itzik decided then, he said, that England was a country full of good, kind people and that he was going to like it. For all the disappointments he had experienced since, he still thought he was right on that Christmas Day.

Whether Itzik recalled what happened accurately in what he told me or whether his memory had turned it all into a story I do not know. But there was a real rabbi, Rabbi Unterman, who was in due course told of his plight. He got in touch with a friend in London, Stencl the Yiddish poet, and between them they eventually got Itzik to London.

For the rest of our time in Edinburgh I am afraid we treated the Congress occasions rather casually. There were some bizarre episodes in the course of the Saturday's business, mostly occasioned by the traditional Scottish pleasure in argument and vigorous dissent and by warring views of national and international politics. On the Sunday morning we inspected Edinburgh Castle with that mixture of reverence and flippancy which the past in a sightseeing context usually inspires. I rather think that our subsequent search in a hansom cab for a pub which would serve us drinks was more to Itzik's taste. Eventually we were able to establish ourselves in a suitable bar as bona fide travellers. All his life, Itzik said, he had been moving from place to place and never till now did he realize he was a bona fide traveller. Austin Clarke and Con Leventhal from the Irish P.E.N. were with us. Ever since the Scottish sea captain, Itzik had been determined to like the Scots and he had forgiven the claret cup by setting against it the Bell Inn's whisky. Now he drank *Brüderschaft* to the Irish as well. This was important for him because, though he delighted in the diversity of nations, he passionately longed always to believe that all men were brothers.

There was a special reception on the Sunday evening at the Royal Scottish Academy but it was not fraternally informal enough for Itzik, or for me. So we resumed our bona fide role and drank in some hotel with a strange band of Scottish Nationalist–Communist–Catholic–Jacobite writers and painters; though nothing seemed strange to Itzik, especially if it were strange.

By Monday, however, he was taking the Congress seriously again. In spite of his strain of fecklessness, he had more than a little of that Jewish regard for intellectual gatherings and he was also anxious to do nothing that would bring Yiddish literature into disrespect. He felt in some sense its custodian and he must not allow it to be slighted either in itself or in his person. At this time, I gathered, there was a sort of rivalry between the two great Jewish languages, Hebrew and Yiddish. Many felt that the future lay with the former, the official language of Israel. Yiddish was associated with the dying, the murdered, past. So for Itzik any threat to Yiddish was a threat to his poetry and his special piety— the memory of those great audiences who had now been swept away to death and of whom he remained perhaps the only memory, the only voice.

From this conflict came, I fancy, a curious duality in his behaviour, in his character. With me and with the other non-Jewish writers whom he met he was trusting and indulgent. We could tease him, advise him, crack jokes with him, and he was relaxed and quick to understand that we were really treating him as one of ourselves. There was no question of his standing on his dignity, still less of injured dignity.

With his Jewish colleagues, on the other hand, he seemed to be touchy, quick to suspect a slight or veiled criticism, even when neither was intended, and rather unreasonably exacting even where he had plenty of evidence that they admired him and wanted to help him. I met them only through him and saw very little of them: they did not belong to my world and I tended to dismiss them, no doubt unjustly, as a familiar type of *conférencier* for whom I felt indifference rather than hostility. My impression, probably wrong, was that they were concerned lest I be leading Itzik into dissipated ways or at least not discouraging tendencies in him of which they disapproved. I am sure they meant him well and were anxious for his good. After all, they knew a great deal more about his background and his failings than I did at that time, and the Jewish respect for temperance in the use of alcohol is sometimes so strong that it rather exaggerates the weakness of anyone in breach of it, especially if it is a weaker brother of the same faith. That Itzik himself was nervous and self-conscious on this score one may perhaps infer from some of his poetry.

For, during the time I knew him, one would not have described Itzik as temperate—nor would he have sought that description. Not that he was an alcoholic either. But he was at all times excitable, and alcohol made him more so; he had rather a weak head and so got drunk on what would have affected others comparatively little; and he enjoyed the company of drinkers and the social pleasures that go with drinking. I suspect also that, like other imaginative writers who have passed their first lyric spontaneity, he valued the stimulus alcohol can give to the imagination, the access to paradox, unexpected simile, dislocated association. And he may also have needed it for escape from his often acute consciousness of a past and a people utterly destroyed, a youth which had gone for ever not as the youth of most people passes, to be recalled, sentimentalized, and cherished among the survivors of one's own generation who share it, but lost for ever with the generation which had no survivors.

Itzik had asked to be allowed to give a paper on the Yiddish theatre for the session on the Wednesday of that week and he was much preoccupied with this in the days beforehand. He had it in mind especially to reinforce Joseph Leftwich of the London Yiddish Centre in drawing attention to the persecution of Yiddish writers in Russia, some of them friends of himself and of Leftwich. This paper was of great importance to him, not so much for his own sake as for that of these friends and for his anxiety that people should know about Yiddish drama and share his pleasure in it. He constantly went over with me the line he proposed to take and discussed various ways of putting things; not so much because I could be of any special help to him, given my ignorance, as because he was nervous of his English and because this was not the kind of audience that he had known so well how to master and make his own.

When the session came, however, Itzik was low down on the schedule of those due to speak, the speakers before him were as voluble and unconscious of time as writers usually are on these occasions, and the chairman was too sparing with his gavel. Itzik grew unreasonably, though understandably, fretful as people began to drift away before his turn came. Eventually, gesturing and shrugging his offended impatience, he stalked out, his unread paper in his hand. I followed him. As he wrote to me later, 'I did not read my paper simply because I left the Hall as a protest at being called up when the Hall was nearly empty, you came with me and we had a drink together, you agreed that to speak to empty walls I need not come to Edinburgh!'

He was indeed very upset and I tried my best to comfort him. I had to overcome my own feeling that such trifles weren't worth worrying about, and that speeches in any case achieved nothing, by reminding myself that I came from a more easy-going world and that my companions and friends and family had not been murdered or put in danger of murder. I did rather suspect that there was some residual vanity resentful even in a spirit as great as I by now knew his to be and that in the back of his mind he must have been grieving that he was in a strange country where the name Itzik Manger meant nothing and the subject of Yiddish Drama was too obscure to excite interest. But there was also the fact that he had meant to close with an impassioned plea on behalf of the writers then silenced, if not worse, in Russia and he regarded himself as having been robbed of a chance of doing his small best to help them. And I guessed he was worried lest his colleagues might think he had defaulted out of mere pique or irresponsibility or simply because he wanted to go and have a drink.

There was nothing for it, however, but to console him and assure him that he had been right but that he had best forget about the whole thing: one good poem was worth an infinity of lectures and even if he had spoken with the tongues of angels the results for Yiddish drama or his persecuted friends would have been precisely nil. I privately hoped that his colleagues would blame everything on me, if they worried about it at all.

From this incident, however, I learnt that Itzik could be passionately sensitive to the point of being unreasonable, that he lived in two worlds: the one he shared with me and people like me, and the one he shared with his fellow Jews. His ties with this second world were the more profound, even though he might like some of its inhabitants far less than he liked some of us. For it was a family world, a world of shared experience, shared suffering, which transcended the lives and experience of any one generation because it was rooted so deeply in the age-long past of his people.

Yet, given his situation and his temperament, it was a world he was bound to fret against. For he was intimately dependent in the last resort, not on us his casual Gentile friends, but on his fellow Jews, those with whom he was thrown together because they were all in the same rudderless waterlogged boat. And his dependence was bound to make him unfairly critical. There was a pride in him like Dante's, which bitterly resented the climbing of other men's stairs, the Dives–Lazarus relationship to which the unworldly poet is so often doomed and indeed dooms himself; and doubly so when he is a refugee and must look to others for the understanding of his work, even though it may be only his language they understand and not what he is trying to say, the vision he wants to express, the special self that is the vision's only medium.

There were other episodes in Edinburgh more cheerful for him. We went to see the Festival production of *Bartholomew Fair* and he delighted in that rough comedy, so close in many ways to the people, a sure approach to his appreciation. Discussing it afterwards I was surprised to find how much he had come to know of English literature, not only of the dramatists and the obvious Romantic poets but of less expected names. It was only much later that I learnt of his poem, 'The Ballad of the Dying Christopher Marlowe and the Jew of Malta', and another, 'The Song of Jonathan Swift and the Yiddish Rhymester Itzik Manger'; but they may not have been written at the time I met him. Even then, however, he showed a particular feeling for Swift, a feeling I shared, and now that I knew a little of his powers of resentment and invective I wasn't surprised.

We ended the conference where we began it, at the Bell Inn, cutting on that last night the formal dinner of farewell, because we feared the speeches, and talking instead of the sad fate of the Pakistani member who had brought with him to Edinburgh a vast sheaf of poems and was baffled because no one would listen to him reading them; or the charming lady from Turkey who never ceased to discourse of the spirit of Anatolia and thus unconsciously defended herself against the endless overtures of men who wanted to understand Anatolia in a more carnal and desirable form.

In a diary entry made about a month later—there had been an interval too busy for punctual journal-keeping—I noted: 'Itzik Manger, the Yiddish poet, the only convincing person I met of the first class. His passion for whisky, his inability to refrain from smoking in the dining-room . . . and the famous speech on the Yiddish drama.'

In the meantime I had had a letter from Itzik with thirty shillings I appear to have lent him—for a poet of his penury he was unusually strict in the repayment of loans, a characteristic I found as agreeable as it was unusual. He was to dine that night with John Willett, a friend to whom I had introduced him in Edinburgh, when John and Erich Kästner were like ourselves in flight from oratory. Itzik's letter reported that Con Leventhal had written about the dinner we had failed to attend: 'The Turkish woman who behaved so nicely as chairman spoke so endlessly about the soul of Anatolia that the soul of Anatolia haunts him even now in Dublin he does not know how to get rid of it!'

Itzik at this time was looking after the German section of a bookshop in Swiss Cottage which belonged to Miss Margaret

Waterhouse. He had met her in his early days in London and she had introduced him to various writers—Arthur Waley, among others—and taken a very active interest in his health and welfare. Indeed, by all accounts only the term 'ministering angel'—angels were not just clichés in Itzik's world—suffices for the part she played in his life during his London years. At their first meeting she had discerned his special quality and thereafter did her best to look after him and dissuade him from ruining his health through drinking and smoking too much and allowing his irascibility to spoil his prospects with people who wished him well.

Some time in September I met him in London, probably in a Bloomsbury pub, and introduced him to my wife. We went on afterwards to a party in Coram Street. Early in October he wrote to me again: 'I am very glad to have met your wife, I did not imagine before that she is so friendly as I found her, but I am glad it happened so.

'To tell the truth I felt very uncomfortable on that evening, for the simple reason—I did not know how to behave myself—you were bantering me . . . all the people round were strange to me—although kindly, so I couldn't do anything but spill some of my whisky on the skirt of the lady you were seeing off to New Zealand!

'I am sorry, not for the ladies skirt, but for the two glasses of whisky!!

'I hope to see you and Winnie soon and to have a real good chat with you.

'I have read one of your books so I know something about you, but you do not know anything about me—I would very much like that you should.

'I hope that when I can invite you and Winnie to the celebration of my fiftieth birthday in Paris, you will come as my guests.'

Imperceptively, I didn't think there was anything here that called for a reply and I dislike writing unnecessary letters almost as much as writing necessary ones. I was wrong not to have replied—I still didn't fully realize how sensitive Itzik was. A few days later I received a letter from his friend, Margaret Waterhouse, written without his knowledge. He had got it firmly into his head, apparently, that I was offended with him and he was in a state about it. 'He is silly if he drinks and maybe he was rude—he really is too excitable.' She asked me to send him a friendly note. 'He is not very happy, and has suffered much. . . .'

It was imperceptive of Itzik too, of course, to imagine a man I liked as well as I obviously liked him could have offended me. And in any case my vanity is so carefully camouflaged and surrounded by such defences in depth that even I sometimes lose sight of it or forget the way in. But I was too painfully familiar with that combination of guilt and amnesia not to remember what fantasies of one's own bad conduct it could elaborate. So I wrote to him at once. I probably told him that I'd had too much to drink myself to remember what he might have said or done and was in any case certain that there couldn't possibly have been anything for any sensible person to take offence at.

His reply was by return. 'I was really afraid that, through my drinking too much, I did upset somebody, and least of all I should like to upset you, but God Bless Bacchus, the discoverer of Irish whiskey, who made you as drunk as myself, and I hope the rest of the company!

'You may be sure that I should like to see the tribe of Dan, and maybe I shall tell you about the greatest Yiddish writer Sholom Aleichem, who created one of the outstanding characters in world literature, called Tevye, the Milkman, such a sentimental philosopher who was blessed only with daughters, there was seven of them, and what beautiful daughters they were! I must tell you about them. Surely, there are translations of his works in English, but very bad ones, because Yiddish is such an idiomatic language that in taking away the idiom it loses all.

'I will take the earliest opportunity to meet you, your wife and your daughters, and if you will have patience I will read you some of my work. You remember the Pakistan delegate who brought up to Edinburgh all his manuscripts looking desperately for someone to whom to read his poetry. That poor dear could not understand a Congress of writers who should not be interested to know what one of their delegates are writing. I can't say exactly that I am in the same state, eager to communicate to anybody some of my poetry—some of my most intimate dreams, but I must confess I would like to read some to you. In the ten years I have been here I have only read some of my works to Margaret and to Arthur Waley, who would very much like to see them translated into English.'

I had already in my letter invited him to our house in Oxford for the next possible week-end but he had a cold and put it off until 28 October. 'I wouldn't like to bring my London-germs to Oxford and infect the tribe of Dan. I would feel worse than Raskolnikoff for that crime.'

I happened to be in London that Saturday and I brought him down with me—he was always nervous of going anywhere for the first time and one had the feeling with him as with Dylan Thomas that unless carefully, though unobtrusively, shepherded he would go astray. The visit was a great success for everyone. Like many men with no children of their own he was, in the innocent sense, a natural father. He especially delighted, and delighted in, our three daughters Anna, Delia, and Brigid, then aged ten, seven, and five. He understood at once the complexities of our extended family: the aloof but benevolent dignity of Big Cat, the frivolity of Kitty and her suitors, the emotional exactions and charm of Katie the schnauzer, and on the canal the remoter dependency of the ducks and the frieze of swans. He had a vast repertory of stories, many of them about animals, that had one level of meaning for children and another for adults. He saw fables in everything and his parables were innocent of that terrible literary frigidity, were still as fresh as those of the New Testament and drawn as directly from the surrounding life.

He was adept at all kinds of simple conjuring tricks and he loved disguises. A favourite act was that of the tall, dark stranger. We would be sitting at supper, except for Itzik, with curtains drawn and the fire alight. There would be a loud knocking at the dining-room door. I would call 'Come in'. The door would open slowly and a stranger, about eight feet tall, would come in backwards, wearing a long black overcoat and with a black hat on his head. The children would shiver with delicious horror, Katie would growl and Big Cat would tense. Even my wife and I, though recognizing my London overcoat and my bohemian hat bought in Montparnasse years before, would feel a sinister *frisson*.

Then the stranger would turn to face us and, like some death figure of medieval allegory, would disintegrate. The overcoat would open and reveal a diminutive Itzik and he would lower the broomstick of which the broom end had formed the giant's shoulders and supported the headless hat. His pleasure in our pleasure, and his pleasure in having been for a few minutes a frightening giant, was the crown of it. The children would make him do it again, with the same result, except that Big Cat had become blasé. And from then on this turn was a compulsory prologue to every evening meal.

The last night of his stay with us was Guy Fawkes Day. Catholics though my wife and I had been, we felt that this celebration had in the religious sense at least been defused and so, to amuse the children, we always had a bonfire and fireworks where our garden ran down to the bank of the Oxford Canal. This Sunday night all was at first much as usual—catherine wheels spinning on the trunk of an apple tree, rockets sibilating towards a brilliant explosion in the sky, roman candles like Nero's Christians stoutly burning, and children standing with sparklers at alternately rash and respectful distances from the fire. Itzik was in his element, holding Brigid with one hand and a sparkler in the other, his face lit up by the fire without and a radiance within. One of the children lit a jumping cracker which in three testy hops jumped into the box of fireworks. Unscheduled explosions began. I sprang across to retrieve the bigger bombs we had been saving for a grand finale. Itzik pushed Brigid backwards as he leapt in front of her to save her from any flying bombs. She fell in a patch of nettles but appreciated Itzik's heroism too much to tell him or to cry. Ever afterwards she remembered him with a tingle in her bottom as well as in her heart—though she told him only of the latter.

When everyone else had gone to bed that night he and I stayed up late. He read me some of his poetry, first in the Yiddish and then in a rough extempore translation of his own. I knew no Yiddish, of course, but felt moved nonetheless by the voice, so vibrant and flexible and passionately eloquent. And his translation, however imperfect the English, gave me an idea of the matter of his verse, the themes, the mastery of homely metaphor, the easy power to move familiarly between the everyday and the sublime. I sensed in him something of a Yiddish Villon, of Nerval, of Rimbaud. I suggested to him that he was doing with words what Chagall was doing with paint and I found that he was pleased: for he regarded Chagall as a master and a kindred spirit.

We talked then and he told me of his beloved brother crippled in battle at Stalingrad and deported to Central Asia where he died of illness and hunger; of his sister back in Romania at this time and besides himself the only survivor of the family; of his dead mother and his father dead also, dead in the concentration camp where the Nazis had dragged him.

We talked about fathers and I told him about my own father, so much more fortunate than his, an immigrant to New Zealand and a man who had also lived by hard work and his hands, an Irish speaker who like Itzik had lost the background in which his first language made sense. I told him also of Larry Hynes, another immigrant to New Zealand and an Irish speaker, a wandering story-teller like Itzik, a *seanachai*, one of the last of his Irish kind, who had travelled on his bicycle round the Irish farms of Southland and on winter nights, in front of fires made of totara or Black Diamond coal, not turf, had made us shiver with his tales of ghosts and shape-changers, and fairies stealing little children to leave changelings in their place, and magic warriors battling in the evening clouds, and revenants from fairyland who had lived a hundred years in the course of a day and a night of fairy love, coming back to cold ashes, cottages of fallen stone, and new un-remembering generations.

In return he told me stories of the *schnorrer* and the rabbi, of beggars and mountebanks and robbers, of wise cockerels and speaking animals, interweaving into these anecdotes of peasant memory Biblical references so absorbed into his subconscious that they came out transmuted, remoulded, and so natural a part of his narrative that one had a sense of timelessness, of eternity, and recurring names like Abraham and Isaac and Jacob sustained the long centuries through which so many succeeding men, fathers and sons, had borne them and the customs of their forebears.

Next morning I set off to the office, leaving Itzik at the breakfast table somewhat dejected and showing little sign of appetite— the result of the whisky with which we had stoked our enjoyment and our imaginations the night before, and of too little sleep. Brigid was worried lest he feel hungry later when he was on his way back to London. As he was leaving she presented him with a hazelnut so that he would not starve.

Punctilious as I was always rather surprisingly to find him, he wrote a day or two later to thank us. 'Because of the marvellous thing that happened to me!', he enclosed for Brigid an unusual sort of bread-and-butter letter—lost, alas, because she was so enchanted with it that she took it to school to show her friends, and her teacher borrowed it. Itzik had been sitting in the railway compartment on his way to London, it seemed, and he had indeed felt hungry. He couldn't afford to go to the restaurant car. He remembered the nut. It would be better than nothing. He cracked it. A fairy appeared, for it turned out to be a magic nut, and gave him three wishes. He wished for roast beef, cabbage, and potatoes—what we had had for lunch the day before and Brigid's favourite meal. The fairy waved a wand and there in his lap was a plate of roast beef, cabbage, and potatoes, all steaming hot and with gravy, and there was even a white linen napkin and a silver ring. But then he saw that the little girl opposite him was looking at his plate, hungrily. He asked the fairy to bring another plate of roast beef, cabbage, and potatoes. And there it was suddenly, on the little girl's lap. But now the little girl's mother was looking hungry. So he used up his third wish, as the best of men always do. The third plate appeared. They all ate up everything on their plates. And then the plates vanished, and the napkins, and the silver rings, and the fairy vanished also. And all three of them were very happy. They didn't even have to wash the dishes afterwards.

We met a few times in London between then and Christmas and I tried to introduce Itzik to people who might prove helpful —he was, of course, very poor and it is hard to see how he would

have survived at all, frail as he was, without the help of a few
devoted friends and especially Margaret Waterhouse. To remind
me of our talk about Chagall he sent me for Christmas the Tate
Gallery postcard of Chagall's '*Le Poète Allongé*'. 'Look at the
painting of Chagall and imagine yourself in it with all the girls
and that's that.'

Writing to me early in January he returned once more to the
subject of the P.E.N. conference, in some agitation. He had for a
long time now been trying to get invited to lecture in the United
States, and especially in New York, so that he could be among his
own people again. For this reason it seemed to him that his relations with the Yiddish P.E.N. Club in New York were of great
importance. He began to suspect that their failure to facilitate a
visit by him might have been caused by someone's having given a
misleading account of the occasion in Edinburgh when he had
refused to read his paper. So he now asked me to write to the
president in New York and give an objective account of the whole
episode.

I knew how easy it was for a man of Itzik's temperament and
desperate isolation to put a somewhat paranoiac interpretation on
little or no evidence and guessed that at most and at worst some
bit of émigré gossip had become inflated in the usual way—
shades of poor Herzen and his friends. I was not inclined to attach
very much importance to Itzik's story except in so far as he
believed it and was upset by it. The delays were sufficiently
explicable in terms of the bureaucratic suspicions felt by the
American authorities towards any penurious European intellectual trying to infiltrate the last bastion of capitalist democracy.
And if, over and above this, some pettiness or malice had been
operating against him, common sense would be bound to triumph
eventually. Most people, after all, are basically sensible and even
generous; and if they aren't it is less wearing and in the long run
more effective to behave as if they are.

I cannot now remember if I wrote to the president but I very
much doubt if I would have thought it a helpful thing to do. At
any rate, I heard no more from him on this theme, though I
resolved to be on the watch henceforth for this touchiness of his

and to do what I could to build up in him the self-confidence to
which his marvellous talent entitled him—always remembering
at the same time that his irritable pride was part of the talent and
perhaps one of its necessary conditions.

My next letter from him was written in Paris on 21 January
1951. Some celebration had as he promised been arranged there
to commemorate his fiftieth year but my wife and I had been unable after all to accept his invitation. Instead, I had given him an
introduction to my old friend Paddy Costello, at that time New
Zealand's First Secretary in Paris, and his wife whose maiden
name was Lerner and who had grown up in the Yiddish-speaking
quarters of London's East End. 'Greetings and love for you, for
Winnie and the three girls. Costello sounds Italian but he is *Irish*.
We drank Bruderschaft. Hope to see you and Winnie in Paris as
soon as possible.' And Paddy had appended a postscript. 'Manger
and I met for the first time this evening at my place. I hope
to see him many many times again. He doesn't eat, which
is curious; but he can drink, glory be to God, and in one
moment I shall be keeping him company in some claret. *You
must come here.*'

As Paddy was himself a splendid linguist with a beautiful Irish
tenor voice and a repertory of songs in every European language
and was my favourite friend from old days in the Western Desert,
I was sorely tempted but too tied to my work in Oxford. Itzik
came back in mid-February and wrote to propose a visit to us two
days later, on 17 February. 'I hope you have got Mr. Costello's
address. I owe him a very long letter for that beautiful reception
he arranged for me at his home. I do not forget that the instigator
of this reception was you. . . . I look forward to seeing the
smashing girls.'

This reunion with the family was as successful as the first meeting had been and once again the tall, dark stranger appeared at my
daughters' imperious demand. When the time came to leave I got
him a lift back to London with a friend. They ended up in the
Black Lion in West Hampstead and my friend promised to try
and arrange for him to give a talk to the Fabian Society on Jewish
folk-lore. This came in the end to nothing. Another similar ploy

of mine failed. Finding that Itzik and Isaac Deutscher had known each other in pre-war Warsaw and that Isaac shared my view of his genius I put them in touch with each other again. Isaac tried to arrange for a broadcast by Itzik on the Third Programme but the BBC decided there was not much point in having Itzik talk in his incomprehensible English about poetry which 'nobody' could understand anyhow.

It was during this period that Tamara, Isaac Deutscher's wife, first met Itzik and she still recalls the 'phantasmagoric tale' he told her when they were walking from Swiss Cottage to Haverstock Hill: the story of a cock, resplendent in flaming plumage, suspended over the home of the Deutschers and strident with the joy of life when it saw Itzik walking with Tamara. She remembers also that the Polish poet Antoni Slonimski translated one of Itzik's poems, one which he had recited to me already in Oxford, the story of a little bird whom a tender and loving mother tried to protect against the winter frost by wrapping him in many shawls and scarves. The shawls and the scarves were so tight and so heavy that the bird could neither sing nor fly.

Back in London after his visit to us, Itzik wrote: 'I enjoy very much the "American Anthology" that you gave me, or I had better say that I took away from you! My conscience is not clear in this matter, but poetry is a great temptation to me, so please forgive me.' And to be sure of being himself a giver he sent me three volumes of Chekhov's short stories. 'I will send you one of these days the translation in French of my "Ballad of the White Bread" that I want to dedicate to you.'

But now at last his own efforts and those of his friends were having some effect. He had from time to time published in Yiddish magazines in the United States and his visit to Paris may well have been the result of an article in a Paris Yiddish paper which had asked: 'Where is Itzik Manger? A great Yiddish poet has vanished. What has happened to him?' Now he had been found again. On 14 March 1951 he wrote that he was leaving for Montreal a week later, *en route* for the United States. 'I hope to earn some money with my lectures and recitals I need so badly. I take your novels with me. . . . I hope to be back in June or July with cheerful pockets, and a less troubled soul because of those damned Volpone-matters.'

In New York Itzik found friends and some of that lost audience which England and devastated Europe could no longer provide. He did not return that year, but we corresponded in a desultory way and he sent postcards to the smashing girls. I wrote to him early in 1952 to tell him I would be in and out of New York in March and April. In his reply of 6 February he explains that he is off to a sanatorium near Philadelphia 'to save a bit of my health'. He wanted to arrange a reception for me at the Yiddish P.E.N. but as I was in for a busy time and had to visit Princeton, Washington, and Toronto, all in a few short weeks, I had to decline.

We managed to meet some time in April and we had a splendid evening together. He took me to see the old Yiddish theatre in Second Avenue, at that time no longer active, and we dined in a nearby Yiddish restaurant, once the meeting place of all the great men of the drama, and now a rendezvous of ghosts whom Itzik vividly evoked for me from his knowledge of the legend. On the way home, to exorcise his sadness, for he seemed at that time still something of a waif in New York as he perhaps was everywhere, he insisted on visiting every bar till we found one congenial for talking and there we sat till closing time, four in the morning, still travellers in good faith if not bona fide.

We met several times again during my visit. He seemed especially amused because, to cut down on luggage, I had only a single drip-dry shirt with me which I washed every night in the hotel bathroom before going to bed. I think he probably had some exaggerated notion of my importance as a publisher and a business man and found this touch of the frugal and the vagabond quaintly incongruous, belonging more to his world than to the world he imagined to be mine.

One of the things we discussed was the possibility of an Oxford Book of Yiddish Verse and he was enthusiastic for it. But I was unable to persuade my colleagues in New York or at home. Nor could I get backing for another suggestion, this time from Isaac Deutscher, that Itzik, whom Isaac considered an acute critic as well as a great poet, should be asked to write a short book on Yiddish literature.

In the July of that year, after my return, Itzik wrote briefly to tell me he was thinking of having an operation on his lungs and to thank me for passing on a message to Margaret Waterhouse. I delayed my answer rather long and his next letter—it was by now October—once again displays how ready he was to worry. 'I was really upset about not getting any reply.' He went on to tell me that his collected poems were to be published and that there would be one dedicated to me and another to Arthur Waley who, he said, was thinking of mastering Yiddish in order to translate him. 'I am proud of the friendship of both of you although you don't know each other.

'Sure the poems are in Yiddish but I think they are good. Only the good is worthy of the good.

'How I long to see the kids again I am only afraid that when I return Biddy will say to me "Pardon Sir, my name is Miss Bridget".'

He was expecting to be in England in February 1953 after the publication of his book. 'Tell Winnie that she will get drunk, we must take out once for all the wind of her sail. So help me God . . . I enclose some Indian feathers for Biddy but I am looking for some other gifts for the young ladies.'

Late in December he sent a photograph of himself in Red Indian dress, perhaps identifying himself with the members of another lost tribe. By that time his visit to England had been put off and he was hoping to come at Easter in 1954. 'I am longing for a few pints of bitter the same as you did when you were over here.'

But he did not come that Easter and the years went by with the dream continually postponed. In December 1958 a Dutch publisher, at the suggestion of Arthur Waley, sent us a copy of *Het Boek van het Paradijs*, the Dutch edition of Itzik's *Book of Paradise*, in case we would consider publishing an English translation. I consulted a distinguished adviser who knew Dutch well and he reported very favourably on the book but feared the freedoms Itzik's fantasy took with sacred subjects might give offence to orthodox Jews without being acceptable to the ordinary reading public. So yet another of my attempts to become Itzik's publisher as well as his friend came to nothing.

I saw him again in New York in April 1959. The year before he had at last managed to get to Israel, the guest of some literary group. Typically he had written to friends in America: 'For years I've been loafing in foreign parts and now I'm off to loaf about at home.' He had been lionized everywhere during this visit and he was still full of it when we met. I think from now on Israel replaced in his longings the England to which as late as February 1957 he had still been hoping to return. He had written to me then: 'I wish I could visit once more Southmoor Road 103 get sick from booze and the next morning Biddy shall pity me and console me with a magic nut.

'Sure Biddy is Miss Bridget now, the nut's have no magic, the girls are growing their magic fruit will be the apple but not for us old folks.

'Did you get my book? I am translated much in Hebrew, German, Polish. My dream is to be translated into English. . . .

'Please give my love to the Lady of the house, her three daughters. I still remember her modest explanation of the number 103. 1 is Dan 0 that's me, 3 that's my three girls. You must alter the number of your house make it 163 to fit my cabalistical interpretation.

'I hope to see you soon. . . . God bless you all.'

In 1962, he made a second visit to Israel and planted a tree in memory of those murdered by the Nazis. 'Comrades, if you ever see a bird on my tree when I am dead, you must know that the bird is me, my reincarnation.'

We never met again. He did not come back to England and before I was next in New York he had gone finally to live in Israel and been welcomed home like the folk hero of one of his own tales, though not to live for ever, except in fame. He had married the widow of a friend, another poet, and I hope that he found in his home, and gave, the happiness which he brought to the homes of so many others.

He died on 20 February 1969. Here is the poem he dedicated to me, in a translation which draws partly on a version by Paddy

Costello's widow and partly on a collation of my own against the transliterated Yiddish original but which is in the main the work of Isaac Deutscher who, like Itzik, can speak to us now only through his books.

THE EVENING DARKENS

The evening darkens. Evening birds
perch on the twigs. Our life is a miracle
in alien woods. Our dream
takes wing to the stars.

The son's offered sacrifice is long ago.
Dim forms guard the memory
of the knife upraised in the father's hand.
Sweet summer stars tremble in fear.

To the angel only, the marvellously bright one,
who stayed the hand with the upraised knife,
do we cry in the hour of agony
when fate menaces us.

Save us, oh bright one, the killers whet their axes,
drunken lips mumble of sacrifice
but the reek is of murder,
of brandy and of hate.

Old stars fall in the harvest night
spent on the grass. We are young still.
Only a little while ago our forefathers
prattled with the angels.

Like children we read the Bible stories.
Woe to the hand that raises the axe,
the sharp-edged. Ten times woe to the angel
who is late in coming.

The evening darkens. Evening birds
perch on the boughs. Our life
is a miracle in alien woods.
Our dream takes wing to the stars.

Index

INDEX

Ady, Peter, 108
AE, *see* Russell, George William
Aleichem, Sholom, 170
Alexander, Field Marshal H.R.L.G.
  (Earl Alexander of Tunis), 109
Allen, C. K., 93
Allen, Dorothy, 93
Allen, Walter, 94
Ambler, Eric, 12
Arena, 142
Auden, W. H., xvi, 31, 46, 49, 73
Authors, Society of, 131

Bailey, the (Dublin), 25
Balliol College, Oxford, 45–6, 139,
  154, 160
Bartholomew Fair (Ben Jonson), 167
Baudelaire, Charles, 87
BBC (British Broadcasting Corpor-
  ation), xvii, 10, 21, 28, 30, 37, 38,
  40, 47, 132, 142; Third Programme,
  13, 130
Beardsley, Aubrey, 8
Beecham, Audrey, 108, 117
Behan, Brendan, 39
Bell, Sam Hanna, 28
Bell Inn (Edinburgh), 157–9, 160,
  164, 168
Bergin, Osborn J., 34
Best, Richard, 33, 34
Black Horse, the, 47
Black Lion, the (West Hampstead),
  176
Blunden, Edmund, 46, 84, 86
Bodleian Library, Oxford, 115, 118
Bowra, Maurice, 73, 77, 89
Boyce, James, 28
Bricklayer's Arms, the, 5, 42
Brinnin, John Malcolm, 56
British Broadcasting Corporation,
  see BBC
Brogan, Harry, 33–4

Brummel, Beau, 8
Burns, Robert, 160

Café Royal, 55
Cameron, Norman, xvi, 135
Campbell, Roy, xvi, 53, 145
Carson, Sir Edward, 41
Cary, George, 105
Cary, Joyce, xv, vxi, xix, 14–15, 56,
  69–70, 72, 86, **93–120**, 134; *Art and
  Reality*, 95, 107, 115, 116, 118, 120;
  'The Captive and the Free', 113,
  116, 118, 120; Clark Lectures, *see
  Art and Reality*; *Except the Lord*, 106;
  A Fearful Joy, 97, 103–4; *Herself
  Surprised*, 93–4, 101; *The Horse's
  Mouth*, 94, 95, 99, 101, 103, 108,
  114, 115, 116; *A House of Children*,
  69–70, 101; *Mr. Johnson*, 99, 115;
  Not Honour More, 106, 111, 112;
  'The Old Strife at Plant's', 115;
  A Prisoner of Grace, 104, 106; *To Be
  a Pilgrim*, 94, 108, 120
Cary, Lucius, 117, 120
Cary, Michael, 96
Cary, Peter, 96
Cary, Tristram, 96, 118
Cary, Gertrude (Trudy), 94–5, 96, 97,
  100, 101–2, 104, 106, 110, 114, 115,
  118
Caxton, William, 162
Cecil, Lord David, 31, 108, 110, 111,
  119
Cecil, Rachel, 108, 111
Chagall, Marc, 173, 175
Chandler, Raymond, 6, 12
'Character of Ireland, The', 27–42,
  47–8, 51–2, 60, 132, 133, Epilogue
  (W. R. Rodgers), 32–3, 34, 37–9,
  40–2; Prologue (Louis MacNeice),
  33, 34, 57–8
Chaucer, Geoffrey, 126, 162